BUILDING BRIDGES

BUILDING BRIDGES

PHILIP MOHABIR

HODDER AND STOUGHTON
LONDON SYDNEY AUCKLAND TORONTO

British Library Cataloguing in Publication Data

Mohabir, Philip
  Building bridges.
  1. Christian life – Personal observations
  I. Title
  248.4

ISBN 0 340 42589 X

Hodder and Stoughton Editorial Office: 47 Bedford Square, London WC1B 3DP

To Muriel and our family

Contents

Acknowledgments

To the many people who made valuable inputs at different times, playing such significant parts in fashioning and moulding my life, and to all the faithful Christians who supported us over these thirty years of service, I say a sincere thank you.

To all those people in this story whose lives are inextricably linked with ours and without whose contribution this story would never be possible, I pay a special tribute.

To Sarah Mitchell and Eric Morse-Brown who spent many hours patiently working on the draft material I owe special gratitude.

Finally, to Katharine Makower who worked on the final manuscript.

Should there be any credit for this story, it belongs to the Lord Jesus who dealt with me out of His boundless grace, and the whole army of ordinary people who were crazy enough to get involved with my wife and me. My prayer is that as you read it you will be motivated to praise the Lord and be stimulated in your faith to venture and believe God to do the unexpected.

Philip Mohabir

Foreword
by Clive Calver

It was an early morning meeting. I felt excited at the nature of the issues we were talking through. But I was frustrated at the difficulties we faced. Impetuously I burst out, "But the problem is simple, the nigger in the wood-pile is really...!" Then I realised what I had said. I turned and looked at Philip – and knew that already I had been forgiven.

It is not an easy story to share. Yet so often we can find ourselves being carried away by the prejudices of our own culture, and the implied discrimination that is so often present.

It is an enormous debt of gratitude that I owe to Philip. He has loved and cared in such a way as to stimulate and encourage white brothers and sisters to reciprocate the compassion that he has shown to us. I have never known Philip compromise on his 'blackness'. Yet I have seen in him the ability to forgive and to encourage a response despite the hurt and rejection that he has so often suffered. I believe him to be one of the outstanding spiritual leaders of our generation, and am immensely grateful to God for his love and friendship.

Reading this manuscript before its publication has been a unique privilege. To know Philip and Muriel is to love them. To understand their story is to recognise the hand of God on the lives of two very special people. Whether facing the knife or the gun, opposition or deprivation, these two 'saints' have demonstrated an eternal and immutable truth. The Gospel must be

proclaimed in all cultures without fear or favour. And
this they have dared to do in a fearless commitment to
the King and His Kingdom.

The result can be witnessed in new churches and
many lives which have been touched by the Spirit of the
living God. Their story is one of God's faithfulness. Of a
God who loves and provides – in impossible situations!
But it is also the story of a man whose courage in his God
has torn down barriers and overturned prejudice.

In Christ there can be no such thing as Jew or Greek,
bond or free, nor can there be a hierarchy of status
between black and white. We are one Body in Christ
Jesus. Hatred has been met by love in the lives of Philip
and Muriel. Their testimony is a challenge to the
insensitivity and prejudice which is subconsciously
hidden in so many of us. Theirs is a silent challenge to
live as Jesus intended – to see change and reconciliation
reverse the alienation and unfeeling discrimination of
decades.

Among Philip's friends there are many incidents
which could be recalled. They don't appear in these
pages, because they are such that a humble man would
choose not to disclose them. But in writing a foreword
one has the opportunity, like making the speech as the
best man at a wedding, to share some of those things that
one joyfully recalls about a couple. I will never forget
Philip leaning across a dining table to challenge the
Home Secretary with the words "Mr. Minister, my
people need to be heard." In a packed church a
Government Minister was told by Philip, "What this
Government needs is Jesus!" I recall in the middle of a
Spring Harvest celebration both Philip's feet leaving the
ground as he warmed to his themes and continued to
challenge God's people!

There are also deeply felt personal moments, such as
when my youngest daughter lay motionless in my wife's
arms in Philip's house – suddenly taken ill – a moment

when Muriel prayed with a passion and fervour that could only be explained by seeing in the pages of this book how God has led these two in their lives of service for Him.

At a time within our nation when black and white Christians desperately need to discover one another, God has raised up a new generation of black leaders to minister in this country. I praise God for each and every one, for God has sent reinforcements to help us in the battle. Philip and Muriel, along with their family, are in the vanguard of such a movement.

In many ways I trust that this is only the story of the beginning, for a long road lies ahead of us all. God has a unique way of training servants. These pages will challenge and inspire us to follow – whatever the cost – a God who demands our all. Eternity alone will show the results of a life lived in God. In the meantime we can thank God for a black man and his family who have been sent by Jesus to teach us to love one another, and to show us the meaning of service that doesn't flinch in the face of difficulty. I pray that as you read these pages, God will open your heart, as he has opened mine, to understand again that the heart of a nation can be changed, but there is a price to pay. I pray God we will learn the lesson in time to make a difference in our world.

Preface
by David Tomlinson

Philip Mohabir is probably the most remarkable person I've ever met. My first real encounter with him was in the hot and sticky atmosphere of Hairaruni, the co-operative village he and a handful of his friends created out of virgin rainforest. Though Phil is small in stature, I soon recognised that he was a very big man with the ability to march through a whole line of obstacles only one of which could devastate most of us. Here was a man with the capacity to hold any audience of Western Christians spellbound, who could sit with the highest ranking officers in his land and gain their respect and yet who seemed to spend most of his life caring for young men and women in the community and tending their projects with cows, vegetable plantations and saw mills.

One of the clearest pieces of guidance God has given me was that Philip should move to Brixton and work with us in Teamwork. I always knew his influence would go far beyond our borders and it's been a delight to see the extent of God's call on his life.

Perhaps my greatest joy has been to work with Phil on an issue near to both of our hearts: the reconciling of black and white Christians. If the Church is to have any real voice into the appalling racial tensions within our community we must demonstrate unity in a practical way among Christians. It's useless talking and producing papers on trans-cultural unity unless we can actively worship together and share our lives in love and friendship. Few people can walk freely into both black or white gatherings and chide each group for their small mindedness or inherent racism – and bring forth tears of repentance – Philip Mohabir can do this!

We in Teamwork have had the privilege of helping Phil bring the West Indian Evangelical Alliance to birth. He's taken the flak with regard to the WIEA; been told he's racist by some white church papers for beginning a *West Indian* E.A. and suspected of selling out to the whites by certain black brethren. Being a healer of relationships often means being attacked from all quarters.

Apart from his ministry on the level of racial healing, Phil is a vital part of Teamwork's broader task. Our vision is to plant new churches in needy parts of our nation and to help strengthen existing churches, providing the resources to aid each in becoming a powerful force for the gospel. Phil has a truly biblical apostolic ministry. He proved this over nineteen years of church planting in Guyana. He has left behind some eighty or so churches, many pioneered in totally Hindu communities, some in the depths of the bush. Now he joins many of us here in the UK in penetrating our society with the gospel.

But, beyond all the conferences, committees and important tasks Philip participates in, one image of him will stay with me all my life. That of walking with him from his home to our office around the corner in Brixton and watching him readily break off from our intense conversation to talk with elderly West Indian people; asking about their children and their minor ailments and concerns. Whilst others produce papers and debate the technicalities of cross-cultural evangelism and integration, Phil first gets on with the task of loving people.

I'd be very surprised if this book doesn't change peoples lives. It's a powerful story with a challenge to everyone who recognises that God does impossible things through ordinary people who dare to trust him and be courageous.

CHAPTER ONE

"Follow Me": I meet Jesus

"Follow ME and I will make you fishers of men", Mark 1:17. Like a sharp arrow well aimed, these words leapt out from the pages of my text-book and pierced my heart.

It was an ordinary lecture in Religious Education in an ordinary school. I had no particular interest in the Christ or the Jesus person. However *The Life of Christ* was listed as one of the options in the Arts stream and I was determined to obtain my matriculation, so I had decided to study it out of academic interest. I was attending Wray's High School in Croal Street, Georgetown, in British Guiana as it was then. The teacher asked me to read verses 14-19 of the first chapter of Mark's Gospel. As I read, I became aware of a strange Presence and the whole atmosphere changed. The classroom became a holy place. It was as though JESUS stood there gazing down at me. Something different was happening to me. His eyes, gentle loving eyes which went right through me, left me feeling exposed and naked. It was as though time stopped. The moments seemed to hang in the air in one eternal suspense. There was a sweet warm strength and beauty emanating from this person. As He lifted his hand and pointed his finger in a beckoning manner, I could hear a soft yet authoritative voice deep inside me saying "FOLLOW ME...". It was gentle yet irresistible. I was arrested.

What seemed to have been an eternity must have been only a few transient minutes but enough transpired in my heart to turn my entire life upside down. It was a kind of quest command. My ambitions to become a medical doctor and surgeon, my dreams of becoming a practising Hindu priest, my desire to fight for the political and economic freedom of our people were now challenged by the claims of Christ upon my life.

That encounter with Jesus in the classroom began a struggle which lasted three long months. "I was a Hindu, born a Hindu, and will die a Hindu. I do not need any other religion or holy man. I do not need a foreign god, we Hindus have our own gods – actually we have many great gods; is Jesus any more powerful than our Krishna? As a matter of fact, Gandhi the mahatma was no Christian, he was Hindu. He knows best. Furthermore to accept any other religion would be an act of treachery. I cannot be a traitor to my parents, to my religion, to the vedas." No, it was not for me. These and other thoughts went round and round in my head filling every moment with questions and more questions. The search was on. With each passing day the conflict was assuming greater proportions and intensity. Firmly and resolutely I refused to accept that Jesus was the only Saviour, but an unexplained presence lingered. So I tried to play it off, sleep it off, concentrate on my other school work, but deep inside me, I would hear "FOLLOW ME…" In the classroom, in the train, in the fields with the cows, in my bed, "FOLLOW ME…" No arguments, no explanations , no intellectual discourses; just an invitation to follow. Why me?

I sought refuge in our Hindu scriptures, rituals and priests, but I could not escape this loving call. My grandparents were from India. In the 1880s, British Agents had come, recruiting young men and women to become rootless labourers on their many sugar plantations in the West Indies and Guyana. My grandfather

was promised plenty of gold if he migrated and was
assured that within a few months he would return with
enough riches to look after his widowed mother and
other brothers and sisters. They were poor village
people from the district of Gorakhpur. He never
returned, never saw his mom again, never did see his
folks. He died an old man of seventy-nine and was
buried in Non Pareil, East Demarara. He was never
happy, he was a broken grieving man to the day of his
death.

The journey of those early recruits lasted many weeks,
not a few days as was promised. Those who survived the
ordeal arrived weak, sick and disillusioned on the shores
of Guyana. They were scattered to different estates.
They lived in ranges, which were low flat buildings with
roofs made of zinc sheets and walls and floor of clay mud
daubed with a mixture of white clay, cow-dung and
water. There were no streets, no lights, no running
water and no toilet facilities. The ranges were divided
into compartments twelve feet by twenty feet. Each
compartment housed a family. These sugar estates were
established on low mud, undulating alluvial swamp-
land. Mosquitoes abounded, and flies were everywhere.
The families shared their dwellings with the chickens,
sheep and goats. The smell and the lack of sanitation did
not contribute to the health and welfare of the newcomers who replaced the original slaves. Diseases
abounded and the hours of work were long and hard.
Many died of malaria and cholera. I myself was a
malaria victim. Blood, sweat and tears mingled with the
dirt and filth.

They brought their religion, books and culture with
them across the seas. Before long they built temples
which became the centre of their religious and social life.
Our temple was well placed in the very centre of the
estate. It was surrounded with trenches and a pond,
with lotus leaves and flowers. These play a significant

part in our ceremonies. Our temple had its own priest and sadhu (holy man), and even a monkey which reminded us of the great Hanoman god. In the centre of the temple was a beautiful altar decorated with gods and ornaments made of silver, brass and wood. The temple, surrounded by many fruit trees, was my second home. From the age of ten, I had been a student disciple to the priest. Every morning I would attend the rituals and pray with him. He taught me how to give water to the rising sun, how to pray and offer to the gods on the altar. He was my guru and greatly influenced my life, until that day in the classroom.

For three months I struggled and resisted. I would not surrender. Why yield to a foreign God, and risk all that was dear? The more I resisted, the stronger the inner voice would grow. Something strange was happening, a love was beginning to reach me and get to me. My will was weakening, and I did not want to fight this 'Jesus Person'. He seemed so kind and loving. I sought to bargain: "Perhaps I can have a bit of both. Mix it up. Be on both sides," I reasoned in myself.

"Impossible," came the reply. "All or nothing," Jesus demanded.

One evening as I boarded the train for the hour's journey from the city to my village, I sat there alone with my thoughts and became strangely aware of his presence again - loving, warm, holy, very clean. I wanted to reach out and touch the clean air that filled the carriage. That voice was again entreating deep inside, "FOLLOW ME..."

The sun disappeared suddenly into the western horizon, and as suddenly, darkness filled and enveloped everything. I was alone and lonely. In his presence I began to feel uncomfortable. A sense of uncleanness gripped me. Feeling exposed and ugly, I wanted to run away and hide. Slowly I realised that guilt had crept into my consciousness. The feeling grew and grew. Even the iron wheels of the train seemed to grind heavily on the tracks. I was very uneasy. The train by this time had reached my destination. The platform was two miles away from my village. I stepped off that train into the night.

A typical tropical night, hot and humid. The birds had long since disappeared, the last parrot made its noisy departure into the night, beetles whistled and a million other sounds filled the night air. The stars twinkled in all their glory – millions of them suspended like diamonds in the great world beyond. Thousands of luminous fireflies punctuated the thick darkness, silently sparkling and flashing every few moments. Frogs in the nearby trenches croaked in a variety of tones, as a choir blending together, piercing the eerie silence. The animals which had been grazing in the few acres of pasture along the way were wending their way to share their masters' dwellings. All was motionless and dark. Lanterns flickered in the distance as they greeted the weary with a welcome home, even if the house they arrived at was basic and bare.

I picked my way through the muddy puddles, totally oblivious to all else and involuntarily pre-occupied with the sense of NEED. It was as though I was witnessing a play-back of my life – all the lies, the meanness, the things I had stolen, my attitudes, my prejudices. Someone somewhere had made a film of my life and chose this rotten moment to give me a free showing. Each step grew heavier. Step after weary step I felt a consuming fire surrounding me and ready to devour me. I actually felt the pangs of death swallowing me up. Yet in the midst of this I could still hear that voice calling, "FOLLOW ME...." As I came nearer home, I was ready to say, "Yes, I will."

I rushed past my grandfather's house situated three hundred yards from our own and quickly kissed Mom who was still busy cleaning, washing and feeding my six brothers and two sisters. Dad had not yet come home from the day's labour. It had gone seven. He left soon before six in the morning. Mom looked a little bit anxious. I knew that look. I had seen it often. She was hurting for Dad. She would have us make sure that all the chores were done, animals all tied and fed enough water for the morning with enough left for Dad to have a bath, that there was enough wood for fuel to cook. She would have his meal warm and ready. I often caught her with tears on her cheek. She never complained and she never shared the deep secrets of her heart, but I knew she loved him enough for it to hurt. They were not perfect and they were Hindus, but they loved and they were committed. They cared for each other and for us. It was home for twelve. Here we learnt to share the discipline of work and to help each other. We also argued and fought, played and sometimes made an awful lot of noise. It had been sixty years since my grandparents had arrived from India, and two hundred and fifty years since the first slaves arrived. Housing for some had improved slightly by this time, and our family was among the fortunate ones who now had a three-room house built of wood and set on six foot high stilts. Neverthelesss for twelve people it was a real squeeze.

When you are one of nine children squashed in a small space, it is difficult to find a quiet and secret place to pray. So I took the opportunity to lock myself in Dad's room, fell on my knees, and prayed with tears, "Jesus, I will follow you, forgive me, I want to be your disciple. If you are up there somewhere, come to me. I want to..."

I cannot tell you how long I prayed or how many times I repeated myself, but one thing I can definitely say, that I rose up from my knees feeling a great big load had lifted, something new had happened inside me. A sense of peace and joy entered my heart such as I had never imagined. I simply felt changed and happy to be alive. Things would never be the same again.

In the morning I pushed open our board windows to see if the world was still there. It was dawn. Light had penetrated the darkness and soft golden rays of morning sun were infiltrating everywhere. Even the grass seemed greener. There was a softer hue, and a sense of security in the atmosphere. A deep joy and peace possessed and filled me with newness, hope, new horizons of bright tomorrows. I felt like shouting and skipping and dancing. Then I thought – how would I tell my folks what had transpired? A Christian disciple? They would never understand it, or accept it. HELP!

CHAPTER TWO

Battles at home

I decided to be bold and tell it as it was: to nail my flag to the mast, and declare myself a Christian. At first they felt it was a phase which would soon pass. They accepted it philosophically, thinking it was a peculiar search to satisfy my curiosity. They were confident that nothing could overcome my deep feeling of patriotism or challenge my loyalty to my father's religion. When it was clear that my allegiance to Christ was real and that I was determined to go through with my decision to follow him, they demanded, "Change your mind." "Renounce this madness." "Stop this nonsense." When I would not recant, they applied different types of pressure. My own relatives, the community, the whole temple now turned against me. My uncle threatened to beat me – once he came and lifted me bodily to throw me out of the second floor window.

My mother and father were very upset and became increasingly agitated because the neighbours were making them feel outcasts. It was a very close-knit community. These were second-generation migrant people, who had come as slaves or indentured labourers from Africa and India. They all felt as though they belonged and shared a common identity. They related to each other as very close friends. In some cases, they made covenants to accept one another as blood-relatives. The Indian sector of the community especially held their religion in very high regard. Their culture and religion was the cement that bound them together. They helped one another build fences, dig drains, clear new fields, and construct each other's houses. If someone was sick, all seemed to share the problem. Weddings, funerals, religious ceremonies were shared by all, and were always tremendous occasions for a gathering. Their joy, their sorrow, their aspirations were all bound up together. For a people separated from their roots, isolated from their real environment, strangers in a foreign land, alienated, the sense of community provided some measure of security. So my family now experienced great pressure, as their eldest son through becoming a Christian was posing a threat to the whole community, who saw it as a direct attack on their religion and culture. This was betrayal. They felt that I was driving a wedge between friends. The main pillars on which the community was built; religion, culture, and covenant friendship, were being undermined.

Their opposition hardened my resolve and made me all the more determined to follow Christ. I had found a friend in Jesus. He was real treasure. Nothing and no-one was going to take him away from me. None would separate me from him. Beaten, called traitor and impostor, I was now made to feel an outcast in my own village. I realised that it was all or nothing.

One night, the whole village had gathered, as was their custom, for a wake on the night before a funeral. The ladies filled the room, and the men gathered in the yard outside. The place was packed to capacity with young and old. They played games, some entered into light-hearted banter. There were professional singers and mourners. At appropriate intervals coffee and salted biscuits were served. In the midst of all this, the Muslim priest and the Hindu pandit (priest) drew me into heated debate. I was seventeen at the time, and these were grown men, respected leaders in the community; their words were law. They felt that I was very rude and disrespectful even to question their authority on religion. Who did I think I was, anyway? Was I not a simple cane-cutter's son who had grown up in their village? To them it was the height of insolence even to dare question the wisdom of our great and ancient fathers, or suggest that the vedas could be insufficient means to lead anyone to salvation. How can Christianity, barely two thousand years old be compared to their religion's thousands of years in existence? As the debate wore on, I realised there was no way that I could reason with these men. They became angrier and angrier, infuriated because I dared to disagree with their views about God. Their tolerance was stretched to the limit when I declared that "Jesus, the Son of God, is the only way to God. There is one God and one mediator between God and man. No-one can come to God except by Jesus." As the priests turned on me, every other activity ceased, and all attention was focused on the debate. I could sense the temperature rising.

"Jesus is the only mediator between man and God." I stood my ground. I would not compromise. I thought of Peter and John in the Acts, dragged before the Sanhedrin and forbidden to preach Jesus. Spontaneously, almost involuntarily, I shouted, "There is no other name given under heaven among men whereby you must be saved." The priests became angrier, and the people also becoming incensed, turned against me. I felt alone. I looked out on the sea of faces; neighbours and friends, people with whom I shared a common history and destiny, exhibiting rising anger born out of their sense of disappointment and betrayal. Once an apprentice priest who promised so much, now I had chosen to be a Christian. They were perplexed, confused and angry. Hostility oozed with every breath, charging the atmosphere with uneasiness and tension. We were now locked into confrontation. There were more heated exchanges, and I searched in vain for a friendly face. I realised more than ever that I was alone, with no other Christian there or to be found within miles. What to do? Dilemma! Caught in a trap, I reasoned, "Give up or stand uncompromisingly firm and risk your life." Just when I thought they were going to attack me physically, the Holy Spirit whispered, "Challenge them as Elijah did the prophets of Baal."

Fortified suddenly by an inner boldness, I exclaimed rather than shouted, "Uncles, there is no need for us to argue about whose God is real and alive. If your gods are real, let us prove it. Bring your holy books, and I will bring my Bible. We will place them in front of all these people, then you pray first, that your god will send fire from heaven to consume my Bible, and I will pray to my Jesus that he will send fire down from heaven to consume your holy books." A deathly hush fell over everyone. Who was this little upstart of a fellow? But there was such a ring of sincerity and authority in my voice, which I can only accredit to the Holy Spirit helping me, that everybody stood still. I meant every word. By this time my dear father, trembling and fearing that I would come to harm, drew beside me. This was an unexpected strength and support. We stood there, gaze fixed upon each other. Eventually, the priests backed down, saying, "Time will tell." They refused to take up my challenge. The people dispersed and the situation was defused.

Attitudes in my village changed towards me from that night. My own relatives, neighbours and friends decided that they would give me a fair chance to prove whether what I had was real, or whether I was going crazy. Through a series of miraculous happenings which included the sick among them being healed, a church is now planted in my village, and Christians have earned the right to exist among the other people without being harassed.

At school, I was always known as a 'country bum'.

Coming from a sugar plantation, we were not expected
to be up to the standard of the enlightened city boys. We
were despised sons of slaves – a labouring class who
should be content to work in the plantations. The jokes
were cruel and humiliating. Now, when my fellow
students heard that I had become a Christian, they
made me the prime target for all their practical jokes.
They would strike me on one cheek and quote the
scripture, "If someone hits you on one cheek . . . turn the
other." "Prove that you are a Christian". They called
me names: 'church rat', 'holy man', 'reverend'. They
made snide remarks, they mocked, they jeered and
scoffed mercilessly. At times, the embarrassment was
intense. More than once I was made an object of ridicule
in front of the whole school. I did not cope very well at
first; I did not know what to do. I wept many times.
Sometimes I became very angry and wanted to
retaliate, to hit back, but deep inside me I knew I would
be the loser. I had no pastor. There was no church in my
area. I knew no other born-again Christians. There
was no avenue open for fellowship, for teaching or
encouragement. The teacher who was in charge of my
class at school on that first day advised me to go easy,
and not to become a fanatic. However, she encouraged
me to pray and to read the scriptures. I spent most of
my lunch breaks hidden in a corner, praying, and
sometimes overcome by exhaustion, I slept.

I had no Bible to begin with, only the gospel of Mark.
However, the Principal's wife who was white, English,
and a member of the Congregational Church in
Brickham, Georgetown, gave me a lovely new Author-
ised Version. I sneaked it into my father's house
wrapped up in a piece of lace. When everyone else had
gone to sleep, I would light a little bottle-lamp, creep
under the bed, and read page after page like a starving
man. Starting at Genesis, I read and prayed every night
for hours. I do not like to think now what my prayers

sounded like. I am sure they were filled with repetitions and I am sure they would not have made sense to anyone who might have listened. But those hours in the Bible and in prayer were my source of strength. I began to see and understand things about God and about myself that I never knew before. A process of enlightenment was taking place. Slowly and surely, I was beginning to know God. There was a heavenly contact. I received a sense of peace, comfort and strength that enabled me to cope with the temptations and testings and to look at my persecutors and forgive them. I grew to love them. The more I prayed and forgave them, the more I loved them.

I don't quite remember where I got the notion from, but I understood that the early Christians used to pray every three hours. Quite naturally I thought that if I was going to be a real Christian, I too must cease what I was doing every three hours, wherever I was, and pray. One afternoon I was at my uncle's house – the same uncle who threatened to throw me out of the window and to beat this 'Jesus' out of my system . He was not at home at the time. My aunt, although a Hindu and a very simple soul, could see that there was a change in my life and that God was doing something for me. She would give me every encouragement, at the risk of the displeasure of her husband. My hour of prayer had come, and, thinking that I was safe because he was still at work, I sought permission to retreat into his bedroom to spend my hour of prayer. I was there, totally lost in love and admiration, eyes closed, kneeling beside his bed, fervently praying and reaching out to Jesus, when suddenly I was aware that this massive figure was standing in the doorway every inch of six feet tall. I thought – this is it! He was an awfully violent man when he was angered. To my surprise, he stood transfixed at the doorway, and after a while retreated, waiting until I was finished. I was scared to venture out of the room, thinking that this was the height of insult: I, a Christian, praying to my Jesus in his house. Can you imagine then my surprise, when I ventured out of the room, to find my uncle subdued and kindly disposed towards me. Ten years later, he disclosed that while he was entering that room intending to transport me bodily and to teach me a lesson, he was gripped by a mysterious power and arrested – stopped in his tracks. He experienced the presence of my Jesus withstanding him. I noticed a marked change in him. He became my friend from that day on, and later accepted Jesus for himself. How well he followed him, I could never tell, but he remained a professed Christian until he died.

On another occasion, my hour of prayer came round while I was at my grandfather's house. He was a confirmed Hindu, loyal, faithful and true to his religion and his gods. He had been kidnapped and transported across the seas from India as a teenager. I was seized with the need for prayer and while I was praying in a corner of his house, he came in from the fields. He disclosed later that watching me in prayer, he saw Jesus standing over me with his hands outstretched. Jesus met my grandfather that day – although it was much later that my grandfather accepted Jesus. So eventually it came about that on his deathbed, as he drew his last breath, he was heard whispering the name "Jesus, Jesus."

On many similar occasions, when threatened by priests, by angry relatives, by mocking comrades, by people who thought I had done my race and religion a great disservice, time and time again what could have been disastrous situations of great danger for me were avoided by supernatural interventions. I did not escape entirely. I was not delivered from every test, but in the midst of them all I found help and strength to endure and to come out victorious. There were times when I was violently beaten, had to go without food, and was heaped with insults and abuse. There was a price to pay for my faith in Christ. Nonetheless, these hardships all served to bring me closer to him.

In due course this opposition became less and less. The consistency of my testimony, the tenacity with which I pursued my new-found faith, the change in my conduct and manner of life, my willingness to get involved in the practical things around the home and to help my mother and father with the ordinary daily chores confounded and convinced people that Jesus was real and not to be trifled with. I think the most effective weapon, the single factor which changed their minds above any other, was that I did not become sour, bitter, resentful, or show hatred. They were won over by my reactions to their hostility. Instead of anger, I was finding the ability genuinely to love and forgive. The language of love was proving mightier than their belligerent actions. Love never fails. To overcome evil with good is never easy. To bless when cursed, to rejoice when persecuted, does not come naturally, but whenever we find sufficient grace from God to do these things, they yield rich dividends in our lives and become the means by which God transforms us into the image of his Son. Life comes through dying. Conquering by serving and stooping releases a sweet fragrance, extracted from our lives by the act of crushing, a fragrance which spreads and infiltrates the lives of our enemies.

My detractors began to respect me; some of them even accepted Jesus. The most outstanding of these was my dear mother. She first underwent a change in her attitude and thinking when she witnessed a miracle of healing. The youngest of my two sisters lay ill with severe fever and mumps. In those days and in our situation, mumps could be a killer. Now usually when anyone fell ill and grew worse we would seek out the local priest or local recognised witchcraft worker. I myself witnessed occasions when the priest would say his incantations and perform certain rituals before idols for the sick. The local witchcraft worker was different. He sat in front of a brass plate on which rice, hibiscus flowers, incense and cloves were placed. As the incense burned and fragrance filled the room he would shake violently. After a few minutes his voice was different and he would speak things unknown by those present. Another spirit had possessed him. In this state of possession he would cast curses on people, pronounce healing and prepare magic potions to prevent disaster and keep evil spirits away. I knew that sooner or later my mother would turn for help to the only sources she knew. My sister grew steadily worse. I thought, "Lord, I've only got two sisters and we can't afford a doctor. I do not want my young sister to be exposed to such evil influences. You said, if we believe and lay hands on the sick, they shall be healed." So, I laid my hands in simple faith and prayed for the mumps to disappear, and then gave them a good hefty squeeze. To my amazement and my sister's great relief, the fever vanished, and so did the mumps! Mom could not believe her eyes.

I do not recommend this method to everybody, but I was so desperate and my faith was so simple, that I knew my Jesus would not disappoint me. Anyway, it worked, and my mother witnessed her first miracle done in the name of Jesus. She began then to turn her heart to him. Mom was a small woman, barely five feet tall with grey eyes, long flowing hair and beautiful strong yet gentle features. She was a very able person and a good manager. Dad knew her ability and was always content to leave her to manage our meagre resources to satisfy the needs of the family. She was loving and kind-hearted to her children but a very strict disciplinarian – and heaven help you if her anger was stirred! My six brothers and I often felt the sting of the tamarind and blacksage whip across our backs and legs. She taught me how to be industrious, to have respect for my elders, and to have faith in myself. She became very ill in 1953 with a strange fever and afterwards, afflicted with diabetes, never really recovered total health. She used to relate how her parents arranged her marriage with my father, who was a young man in a neighbouring village. She fell deeply in love with him. It was love at first sight. They began life with nothing except a few pieces of clothing and a few pots and pans. It was a tremendous security for us, and for me especially, to see the love and respect and the support that they gave each other in spite of their many ups and downs.

My mother showed no immediate signs of conversion after the miracle of healing, but her attitude to Jesus definitely changed. Gradually she ceased praying to idols and participating in the rituals and ceremonies. Then one day she made an open confession of her faith in Christ. She dared to stand against the tide. She said to me often that she had accepted Christ, although I was never fully convinced of a real regeneration experience. Shortly before she died many years later, I wanted to be absolutely sure. Somewhat shyly I asked her, "Mom, have you accepted Christ?"

"Son, do not be afraid, I accepted your Jesus years ago," she replied, as though she knew exactly what I was thinking. She died two weeks later. I knew Mom had seen the face of the Lord. She is safe in the hands of Jesus.

CHAPTER THREE

"Go to England"

As I mentioned before, I had very little contact with Christians apart from my schoolteacher. I heard that there were some Christians in the city, but never had the joy of meeting any of them, although my school was there. One Sunday in 1953, I made a journey to a village some ten miles away from my house, to visit my aunt. In those days, we either had to walk or take a trip on a locomotive train. We had one single-track railway that ran a sixty-mile stretch between Georgetown and Rosignol, with intermittent stops at every major village. It was great fun and a treat to ride a steam train. As the train pulled up at my village stop, it was very obviously crowded, packed to the doors. I barely managed to squeeze in and hang on. Through that packed carriage, however, above the puff of the steam engine, I began to hear some beautiful singing. As I strained my ears to listen more carefully, the words, "I love Jesus better every day" wafted over the clanging of the wheels and the chattering of the people. It filled me with excitement. For the first time I was hearing singing about Jesus. It was sheer delight. It was music to my heart. I wished I could draw closer to find out who the singers were. They sounded so joyful and sincere; but the train was too crowded for me to reach them.

Once arrived at Unity village, I wended my way to my aunt's house, more than a little disappointed that I had failed to make contact. The strains of that lovely singing trailed behind as the train continued on its journey, leaving behind a cloud of thick black smoke which drifted south-westwards towards the wide open rice-fields. I spent the day with my aunt, and as usual had lots of fun with my cousins after fulfilling my errands. On the return journey, I boarded the train to be greeted by the same singing. This time, the train was not so crowded. Drawing near and sitting at a discreet distance I discovered, as I had suspected, that it was a group of Christians. They had been visiting a nearby leper hospital, to sing and preach to the inmates of that colony. The group of ten were led by one Harry Das. I introduced myself, and before long entered into deep conversation with this dear man. He was tall, with wavy black hair, and immaculately dressed. His eyes were kind but penetrating. He looked happy, with a broad smile and a nice easy approachable manner. I discovered later that he was amongst the very first Hindus in Guyana who had accepted Christ through the witness of a dear lady in James Street, Albouystown. After exchanging the usual niceties, he enquired whether or not I was a true disciple of Christ.

"Are you saved, are you born again?" he asked me. Needless to say, I had never heard these clichés – I didn't know what he was talking about. In my own words however, I related to him what had happened to me three years ago, and sought timidly to tell the story of my pilgrimage since then. He listened carefully, then unashamedly, with tears in his eyes, arms opened wide, he welcomed me as a brother in Christ. I had met my first Christian brother. Through him I met other brothers and sisters in Christ, all of whom had a hand in helping to mould and to shape my early development as a disciple of Jesus.

Through the schoolteacher, through Harry Das, and through my own personal reading, the first two chapters of the Book of Acts became very much alive. A longing and hunger for the Spirit was created in my heart. I wanted all that Jesus wanted me to be and to have. I definitely wanted to be a full Christian disciple. I desired this filling of the Holy Spirit, this Spirit coming upon me, to give me power to witness. It was marvellous – I did not have any theological hang-ups. I could afford to believe what I read, and to accept that it was meant for me as it was for Peter, James and John. In those days, there was a paper called *The Herald of His Coming*, and I was encouraged by Harry to write for a copy. They ran a series of articles on the baptism of the Holy Spirit which made me even more hungry for this experience. I spent most of my days in fasting and prayer, and waited and waited. One night, as I knelt in prayer, I felt an overwhelming sense of God's presence enveloping the room and filling me from the inside. I knew then that I had received him more fully than I had before, although I couldn't define it, couldn't describe or explain it. It was lovely. It was real.

This had an immediate effect on me as a person. I received a fresh revelation of Jesus. My heart melted into liquid love. I wanted to pour out every ounce of myself at Jesus' feet in response to his love. That night I was transported into his majestic awesomeness, and experienced a pure flood of love, holiness and excellence. The High Holy Exalted Christ came down to touch and fill me as he had never done before. It was perfect and delightful ecstacy. I also felt as though I was wrestling with strange and conflicting extremes. I felt rather small as though I was nothing, and yet I felt accepted and uplifted with a sense of goodness. I felt ugly, yet pure and clean as though a bright purging flame was burning me up with an amazing sense of pleasure, weak yet strong, humbled yet happy. I never knew that it was possible to fall in love with Jesus like that. Absolute, total, unconditional unreserved surrender – all these and more cannot adequately express my encounter that night. I ended up one happy heap wrapped up in his love, my bare wooden floor bathed in my tears – Indescribable, Incredible JESUS.

It was not until a few weeks afterwards, when I was praying with the same group of Christians who were with Harry Das in Murray Street, Georgetown, that I suddenly felt an inward compulsion to praise and worship the Lord out loud. Suddenly I found myself speaking in a language I had never heard, learnt or known. It just gushed forth, and with it came rivers and rivers of joy and peace. I felt as though I would burst. I couldn't contain the ecstacy and the dynamism of the moment. I cannot tell how long I stayed in that condition, but almost everyone else had gone home. My friend Harry Das and another companion lingered behind. Wave after wave of this inexplicable presence washed over me. I rose to my feet, feeling clean and closer-drawn. It was as though something of heaven had touched me and come to reside within me. If this was only a taste of what is to come, I couldn't begin to imagine what heaven itself would be like. I was not at any time unconscious; in fact I was very much aware, yet elated and blessed. What I had prayed for – that I should receive the fullness of the Holy Spirit, just as the early disciples did, tongues and all, happened to me without my trying too hard or naming it specifically. It is great to be free of theological debates, and to receive what God has intended to give in any case. He, the Holy Spirit, Paraclete, Comforter, is a gift to be accepted by simple faith rather than to be rationalised theologically.

I was now in my third year at secondary school, and found it increasingly difficult to find the money to pay the fees, to buy books, to get the right clothes and footwear; and on top of all this there was the constant pressure to pay for the train journey back and forth every day. About this time Father sustained an injury to his right foot and was laid off work for months.

Economically, things were not very easy at home.
Having got over the initial shock of my becoming a
Christian, Mom and Dad accepted me and wished me
well, but they could not now continue to support me to
finish my GCE 'O' levels. I really did not know what to
do. So I decided to save some money by cutting out the
train journeys. I would sleep wherever I could in the city
and eat whatever I could find. Sometimes I slept under
buildings. Once I slept in the school-room. Then a kind
gentleman found me on the street and recognised that I
was a country boy without anywhere to stay. He kindly
offered to give me lodging for a few weeks. I spent the
weeks prior to the exams studying under street-lamps,
eating and sleeping rough. For me those exams were a
must. I had a feeling that I needed to equip myself in this
way, whatever the future held.

Then came the exams. I did all the subjects as well as I
could. When the results came, I found that I had done
well – I was overjoyed. "I must share this with Mom and
Dad," I thought. So I hurried home. One glad train
ride. I can well remember as I entered our house
bursting to tell them that I had succeeded. I met Dad
with his right arm almost severed, bandaged up and
hanging in a sling. He was in obvious pain – an accident
at work. I surveyed the scene. Mom was weeping in the
kitchen, wishing she could help him bear the pain and
also filled with anxiety for our future. The whole
atmosphere was subdued, filled with an uneasy
pessimism and gloom. Even my usually lively brothers
and sisters were quiet. My joy now deflated, I chose a
moment to share the news of my exam results.

"God bless you, my son," was all that Dad could
muster. It was enough for me. I wanted him to be so
happy that night. Mom was still overcome with anxiety,
yet embraced me and wept uncontrollably. My brother
George who was two years behind was the only one that
night interested to know my grades. I realised from that

moment that it was time for me to search for employment. I managed to get a simple teaching job in a primary school. It paid me just enough to buy food and give mother a small amount towards the upkeep of the family. Six pounds a month was my salary. Looking back, I wonder how I managed.

It was in that small school-room whilst in prayer one afternoon that I had a visitation from the Lord. I distinctly heard Jesus say, "Leave all, and become a missionary." At first, I thought I was to be a missionary in my own country, preaching round the villages where I lived. Before he showed me where I was to go, he repeated the call once again:

The school was ten miles from the nearest town or civilisation. There was a narrow strip of dirt road with high grass and bush on either side; houses and farmsteads spread along the ten mile stretch. I occupied a small house provided for the two teachers. It was situated about twenty feet from the track and when it rained the yard flooded, as the land was lower than river level. The house was built on three foot stilts. Walls were made of bark stripped from a certain kind of palm tree. The floor had some boards unevenly put together. The roof was thatched palm branches. The toilet was a hole in the ground fifteen feet behind the house, and bathroom facilities consisted of four poles driven into the ground with jute bags hanging to provide you with privacy.

My home village was poor and conditions there were not a lot better, but this was a real challenge to my spirit of adventure. This was new pioneer business. Each family was seeking to eke out a living by growing food and fishing. It was an experience. Darkness would suddenly fall at six in the evening. With no electric light, lessons had to be marked under the flickering light of a kerosene lantern. Reading and study preparation for the next day had to be done under these dim and dull conditions. Mosquitoes abounded and there was no proper drinking water available. We were often entertained by raiding bands of monkeys swinging from tree to tree. The surrounding jungle was never far away, always seeming to encroach on the agricultural clearings made by the settler families. Birds of all kinds, large and small and with marvellous colours inhabited this dense, verdant forest. Their chirping and their singing kept the spirit alive with music and in touch with the God of all creation. I can still hear the silence of those long, dark nights, when I longed for dawn to come and break my loneliness. It was in these surroundings that my Jesus met me again and said, "I want you to be a missionary."

A missionary! I struggled with this calling for three whole months. I was not willing to leave Mom and Dad, my brothers and sisters. They needed steady economic support. As I prayed and resisted and struggled, the Lord gave me this verse: "If you cannot leave mother and father, brother and sister for my sake, you cannot be my disciple." Then I said, "But Lord, how will I be supported?" Back came the answer, "Birds of the field have nests, foxes have holes... consider the lilies. Be not anxious; seek ye first the kingdom of God, and his righteousness, and all these things will be added unto you."

"But Lord, where do you want me to be a missionary?"

"England."

"Oh, no, now I am really going crazy," I thought. "England? Missionary? Impossible! The Queen lives in England! People in England do not sin. It's a Christian country. They do not need missionaries, they send them. England is next to heaven!" Such was our colonial indoctrination.

The more I struggled and the more I argued, the more clear and definite it became that God was calling me to become a missionary to England. I should have known by now not to prolong a dialogue with him. He is always right and he wins in the end. I realised that I was running into danger resisting the Lord. So I sought to negotiate. I said, "Lord, if you provide a passage for me, I will go." Imagine, a passage to London! Although it was only two hundred pounds in 1955, it was an impossible amount for a poor fellow like me to find. So, I thought, this is a good thing for me to bargain with. I challenged God to provide a passage for me in a miraculous way. The more fool I, we never learn. Within a week, I received a telegram from my grandfather, summoning me to his house. I thought, "Now what have I done?" They would never summon me home by telegram unless something serious was wrong. I started on my way home, walking along that long dusty road to Parika, sometimes choked by the dust raised by passing cars. At Parika I caught a bus to Vreeden-Hoop, boarded a ferry and crossed the mile-wide Demerara river to Georgetown, where a taxi ride brought me along more dusty pot-holed roads to find my grandfather waiting.

"Son," he said, "I'd like to give you passage to England." I could not believe my ears. My grandfather! Now old, blind in one eye, feeble-looking. He never even gave me a dollar for a school book, even when I pleaded and begged him at times to help me; he had never given me anything except sweets before. He searched my tired face and must have understood my total astonishment and sheepish gesture. "Oh," he said, "your Jesus, whom I saw that day when you were praying in my room, came to me and said I must give you passage to England. If you pay me back, you pay me back, but Jesus is telling me to give you passage to go to England." He expressed himself in broken English. A miracle indeed. There was no fight left within me. No more arguments. I bowed and said, "Jesus, I will follow you wherever you lead me, no turning back, no turning back."

My parents had a big discussion with the other
members of the family including my uncles and aunts
from both sides. Grandfather was not present. He had
related to Dad what he had experienced. They could
not really understand me. They were not only angry this
time but really concerned because they thought I was
becoming unstable in my mind, that now when my
father and mother needed me most, I was talking about
some crazy scheme for being a missionary to England!
Whoever heard of such a thing? The argument was
going against me, until suddenly I heard my father say,
"I know I have lost my son to Jesus; don't stand in his
way. Let him go, or else we may all have to suffer for
standing against God." Again, God had used a Hindu,
my father this time, to pave the way into the great
unknown for me.

As the time for me to leave drew near, I noticed my
parents busy, cleaning up the house, buying new
curtains, gathering together all the funds they could. I
suspected that something was cooking. Then one day
Mom and Dad took me to Georgetown to do shopping.
We bought a suitcase and packed it with as much as they
could afford. We even bought a new Wilson hat. My
parents issued an invitation to all my relations and to all
the people in the village saying that they were going to
have a farewell party. Then I thought, "God, this would
be an opportunity of a life-time, to witness to everybody
about Jesus."

The night before my departure they all gathered,
packed into every available space in the house and the
yard and out onto the street. At a chosen point in the
proceedings I was to make a farewell speech. With much
trembling, I stood up in that company of three to four
hundred people, Hindus and Muslims, and declared my
faith in Jesus, the changes he had made in my life, the
call he had given me, and that he alone is the true and

living Christ, the only way to God, the only way by whom all men can be saved. I spoke like a man inspired after the first few faltering sentences, transported by an inner might, and strengthened by the Holy Spirit. The audience was stunned; silence reigned. I finished with a prayer of love and blessing, and a benediction on all the families present there. There was a holy hush. God had visited my village and confirmed to the people standing around that what I had found in Christ was not craziness, it was not a fantasy. It was real. He was there, he was real, he touched them and made them know and feel his presence as he had done to me, many times, since that night when I first said, "I'll follow you, Jesus."

I saw how they came, and how they were touched, and how they wept. Then they departed into the long dark night, leaving me with my immediate family. I tried to sleep that night, but even then thoughts of loneliness were beginning to grip me. I was beginning to feel the pain of leaving Mom and Dad: Mother now stricken with diabetes, Dad suffering from his two accidents and injuries, not as strong and robust as before. I lay awake in the darkness of the room, tears flowing down my cheeks. Would I ever see my younger brothers and sisters grow up? Would they suffer because I was leaving? Should I really be so far away from them? England was many long miles away. Never to see them, hear them, touch them; to be unable to help them. I was eighteen, and feeling more than a little miserable. Deep emotions stirred within me, gripping me with a crushing sadness. I fought to regain my equilibrium and some sense of perspective.

It must have been about three o'clock in the morning, when I went out of the house into the yard. I was anxious about my father. He was never a man to share his heart openly. I found him in a corner weeping his heart out. For the first time in my life I realised that there was a deeper bond between my father and me than I had ever imagined. He was my hero. While growing up, I had longed many times that he would throw his arms around me and encourage me and be close to me, but he always seemed so busy, too pre-occupied, too tired. That night I realised that my father did love me. He was going to miss me. Instead of filling me with fear, apprehension and sadness, this made me feel relieved somehow. Relieved because of the knowledge I had now that "My father loves me!" and that there was a bond between us. This gave me a sense of security. I could now go far from home knowing that I had a family who really did care for me. It didn't seem so difficult now to say goodbye.

Morning broke, alive with the crowing of the cocks and activity all around us: people cooking the morning meal and milking cows, the braying of donkeys and cackling of chickens. As the morning sun broke into the night and dispelled its darkness, a new day had dawned for me and soon I would be saying 'goodbye'. Later that morning, we departed for Atkinson airfield – the start of my journey away from home, away from loved ones. As I entered the car, I took a long, last hard look at the house where I grew up, at my neighbours and friends who had gathered round to say farewell, and at the muddy dusty road along which I had trodden so many times coming barefooted from school and from the fields where we often played cricket. A long hard look, and a resolute goodbye.

CHAPTER FOUR

Jesus calms the storm

"We are now boarding." The announcement floated over the laughter, chatter, and occasional sobbing of the milling crowd. Suddenly everyone was moving, shoving and pushing. The hour had come at last. I could hardly believe it. It was really happening.

"Go, my son, and God bless you," I heard my father's voice as he embraced me. His voice was trembling, tears streaming unashamedly down his sunburned cheeks. There were at least twenty-five of my relatives gathered at the airport: brothers, sister, uncles, aunts and cousins. Would I ever see them again? I belonged to them. I was cutting my roots. My identity and my security which I valued highly were here. Thoughts like these assailed my mind in rapid succession. Mother was too overcome with grief to say anything. She looked so frail. But it was as though my heart melted for at that moment I caught the gaze of Jesus' eyes again. They were soft and understanding. I could hear that sweet gentle voice deep inside: "Follow me; trust me to take care of you and of them." It was almost as if he stood at the departure gate waiting. It seemed as though he understood my inmost emotions.

I surveyed the scene. There was noise, confusion and movement everywhere. Sadness hung in the air. Going away from my country was almost like saying a final farewell in those days. The world had not yet shrunken to a global village. London for us was far away. Then came the announcement, "Last call," and I began to edge my way towards the gate, kissing the tear-filled cheeks of my loved ones as I went. Mom looked up briefly as if to say "with my blessing..." This was my own private and personal sending into a brand new world to be a missionary. No pastor, no Christians, only some Hindu relatives who seemed to be caught up in some divine act and will they did not quite understand.

"God bless you, God go with you," they shouted as I neared the steps of the Twin-Otter de Haviland aeroplane that was ready to whisk me away. As I settled in the plane, I discovered that one of my cousins had slipped me a red, gold-nibbed Parker fountain pen with my name inscribed upon it. My Parker and I were winging our way to an exciting new day.

After two hours, we landed at Port of Spain, Trinidad, our first stopping point. I remember thinking what a great relief it was to set foot on terra firma again. My ears were heavy, and I could not hear anyone. A fear gripped me. "O God," I thought, "Am I going deaf?" I panicked. A fellow traveller, obviously accustomed to travelling, gave me simple instruction to relieve me of my misery: "Squeeze your nose, shut your mouth, and blow hard." My ears went 'pop' and instant hearing returned.

After the usual immigration and customs formalities, the few of us bound for Europe were shown to a small none-too-comfortable Chinese guest-house. Here we spent a night and a day while waiting to board a Spanish ship, the *Luciana* – destination Genoa. The ship seemed so long and slim. I had never seen such a big thing on water before. It looked so graceful berthed against the wharf, in down-town Port of Spain. As we boarded I began to feel a mixture of excitement and bewilderment. There were Spanish speaking people, French and German speaking, and a mixture of West Indians from different islands. I was taken down into the belly of the

ship by an attendant. The whole place was jam-packed
with bunks. There must have been hundreds of us,
strangers packed into that dark hole. I couldn't help
thinking of the over-full sheep-pen at home. I soon
resigned myself to the fact that as this was home for a
fortnight, I might as well meet people and make friends.

For the first few days, the journey was a delight; long
hours on deck, plenty of time for reflection and prayer.
By the third day one could not help noticing how people
were getting more drunk, women and men pairing off.
What astonished me was the ease with which grown,
intelligent and obviously influential men in society, on
their way to vacation in Europe, would throw all
caution to the winds and involve themselves in very
unseemly behaviour with young single women on board
ship. These young girls, bewildered on their first journey
as I was, were innocent and ignorant about the ways of
the world. They were travelling to England to study
nursing, take up teaching or law. They could have been
daughters or even granddaughters to some of the men,
who would entice them by much flattery, persuade
them to drink, and then lure them into their cabins. It
was disgusting.

There was lively singing and dancing, but tempers
often flared, especially among the hot-tempered Latin
Americans. As the days passed, the fun was beginning to
wear a bit thin. Jokes became boring. The Caribbean
sun and blue waters disappeared, and the wind became
chillier, the waves bigger. About the seventh day, we
were all awakened by the clanging sound of plates and
cutlery flying everywhere. For two days the dining room
was in total disarray and empty of people. Up, down,
roll. That great big ship seemed like a match-stick on the
mighty ocean. From horizon to horizon, as far as the eye
could see, the waters rolled, under dull grey skies arched
like an endless blanket over us. Women feared that their
last hour was approaching. These same grown men were

bawling in misery, no longer drunk and foul-mouthed, but sober and all of a sudden turned religious. Some found their rosaries. They ran through them faster than I could repeat the Lord's Prayer.

The weather worsened, and the whole ship's population was reduced to a floating sick-house. People were vomiting everywhere. Men and women struggled to keep steady on their feet or else stayed in bed. Rolling this side, then the other side, up, down, up, down and sideways. I felt a little like Jonah down in the bottom of the boat. I stayed in bed most of the time, praying. A group came to me after the third day and implored me to pray for them and for the safety of the ship. I was amazed, because these were the same people who had mocked and scoffed at me mercilessly before, when they learnt that I was a Christian bound for England as a missionary. They had even tried to get one of the younger women to take me to bed. It was serious.

Now I thought, "Lord, this is the opportunity to make your love known to them." My mind raced back to the miracle Christ performed on Lake Galilee, when his disciples panicked and feared that the storm would engulf them. "Well, Jesus, you can do it again." I plucked up what courage I could, and told the people: "Summon up as many as you can on deck." I followed them up after a while, at each step thinking to myself, "You're crazy". On the other hand, I knew that faith was building up inside me. My Jesus is ALIVE. HE IS THE SAME. He is not just history. He did it once, so he can do it again.

Upon reaching the deck a good number braved the elements and ventured out, and I simply said, "God is merciful, and does not desire that we perish. Let us repent of our ways and pray." Then I stretched out my hands to the angry ocean waves, and called in as loud a voice as my courage would permit, "Peace, be still."

I opened my eyes, expecting simply to be laughed at,

but no-one was more astonished than I, when suddenly
the waves receded, and within what seemed to be a few
minutes, the seas became calm and still as a sheet of
glass! We sailed on to Genoa with no further problems.
There was a marked change in a number of people, and
the whole life-style on board was dramatically altered
for the rest of the journey. I found it embarrassing to
cope with all the respect shown to me after this event.
Some began calling me 'father', others 'padre'. I spent
much of my time thinking, praying and wondering what
lay ahead.

We made one stop at Barcelona, where we were let off
the ship for a few hours. It was exciting to go ashore.
This was Christopher Columbus country, the man who
discovered the Caribbean in 1492. You can imagine the
sense of history that filled me when I saw the big
monument in his honour – the ships on which he was
supposed to have sailed to conquer the new world. I was
shocked however, when we were approached by what
must have been hundreds of people begging. It
flabbergasted me to see young children who should have
been in school out on the streets like this with colds
running down their noses, scruffy unwashed hands and
faces. It seemed unreal.

The *Luciana* docked at Genoa after fourteen days. It
was late in the evening, so we slept on board. I
remember the beautiful night sky and the many
coloured lights sparkling on the hillsides surrounding
the harbour: a kaleidoscope of colour which exploded
all around us. Next day we boarded a long, long train
which travelled at an incredible speed through the neat
and picturesque villages of Switzerland and over the
snow-capped Alps. Such scenery, such heights, such
trains and such speeds I had never encountered. But
nothing could equal my joy when at one of the stations
in Switzerland I saw for the first time snow falling, and
was actually able to touch it. The excitement ran

through all the carriages spontaneously, and there were astonished gasps of joy.

The journey over the English Channel from Calais to Dover was uneventful, and everyone became more apprehensive of the future. Some were of course returning home, but most of us were children of the great Empire coming home to the centre of our world for the very first time. We were coming to the mother country, not at all sure what lay ahead of us. And for me, all I had was a promise and a call. I felt an inner sense of destiny. I realised that it would only be a matter of hours now, before I found out the sanity or otherwise of my decision to leave all behind and answer the call to be a missionary to a land which had itself been the centre of missionary activity for centuries. The wind was biting, and it cut straight through my flimsy tropical wear. I shivered. The white cliffs of Dover came steadily closer, reaching out a welcome from the shores of the mighty Great Britain.

CHAPTER FIVE

London, bleak arrival

As my fellow travellers joked with one another, I was preoccupied with my thoughts: "Where will I go? I don't even have an address. Soon everyone will be welcomed upon arrival. Will there be anyone to greet me? What shall I do?" These and other questions pressed upon my mind. Suddenly I realised forcibly the implications of my obedience to the call of God. It was a step of faith into the great unknown. There were hundreds of people around me – yet I felt rather lonely. I whispered a prayer, fully determined to obey the Lord whatever the cost. There was no turning back for me. Arrived at Dover, I boarded a train for London, and gazed out of the window while we sped past towns and villages, seeing the clouds of smoke rising out of a multitude of chimneys to blend with the already dull grey skies.

Eventually the train pulled up, brakes screeched: Victoria Station. So, on 16th April 1956, I had arrived in London. The doors flung open and instantly people poured out onto the platform. It is difficult to describe the scene, with relatives and loved ones who had not seen each other for years suddenly shouting and embracing one another, some laughing, some weeping. The warmth and joy of the occasion can hardly be captured in words. I stood there alone with my suitcase, feeling rather out of it all. As I beheld the joy, the ecstacy of people reunited after long separations, I pondered

again, "What shall I do?" I picked up my case and made
my way towards the exit, still looking around
occasionally, wondering "Did God send someone to
meet me? Would anyone recognise me?" Unfortunately, there was no-one.

I came out of the station and crossed the street. I stood
on the pavement with my luggage beside me. I looked
up at the Grosvenor Hotel and felt in my pocket, but
realised that there was no way that my £10 would buy
me a night of shelter and warmth in that great big hotel.
I felt cold and overwhelmed. It was the middle of the
rush hour, with thousands of people milling back and
forth. Buses with two stories – double-deckers –
buildings that reached into the sky, cars, people, buses
and coaches all mingled together in one mass of
perpetual motion and activity, and I stood there feeling
cold, frozen to my bones. I didn't realise that it could be
so cold. Dressed in simple tropical clothing, I couldn't
feel my nose and ears. My feet were like two lumps of ice.
Instinctively I cried, "God, where are you?" and then I
prayed on in desperation.

"I am here, God, at your command. If I die here, I
have the satisfaction of knowing that I obeyed you. At
least I die in obedience. But if you have a plan, a purpose
for me in this country, please give me a place to sleep
tonight." Having prayed, I opened my eyes, and a man
came rushing out of all that milling crowd, pointed at
me and shouted, "You there, have you got a place to
sleep tonight?"

"No Sir," I replied. "How do you know?"

"Don't worry about that," he said. "Come here.
Have you got any money?"

"Well, Sir, I have ten pounds."

"All right," he said. "Just follow me."

I followed him, and he promptly placed me on a bus,
paid the conductor my fare, told him where to put me
off, and said, "On your left after the bus stop, go to this

street, knock at this number and tell them you need a place to sleep tonight." Just like that, and he vanished into the crowd! Whether or not he was an angel, I shall never know. But I did as he instructed, and sure enough, at the other end of the journey, somebody welcomed me in, and assured me I could stay there that night.

That is how I made my entrance into Britain on a cold April evening. The clouds were grey, and the atmosphere was heavy. I spent my first night at this strange house, with people I had never known ... After waiting for about five minutes in the entrance hall, which was rather bare, a man with a friendly smile and a very concerned look ushered me into a room and pointed to a sofa in the corner, saying, "You can have that as a bed for the night." I could actually see the springs making their way through the upholstery. I looked around and thought, "This can't be true!" The walls were damp, the wall-paper torn and hanging, the rattling windows were dirty and covered with soot; there were no curtains and a solitary light-bulb hung from the ceiling, its light hardly reaching the far corners of the room. There were several double bunks, with no covering, and in between them there were chalk marks on the floor. There was nothing else except my little sofa.

The evening grew colder, and darkness soon enveloped everything. Street lamps and lighted windows punctuated the darkness as if to remind one that all was not dead. The room filled up with men who must have been permanent residents. They washed themselves in little enamel basins by their bedsides. As they did so, they recounted the adventures of the day, some of them very sad tales. These were men who had left families, friends and home in search of improvement, who were now landed up in a situation where they were almost paupers. I saw grown men weep openly that night. They could not write back to their families: they had no money to send to maintain them. Pride would not allow them to relate their failure to find work, or find a home, or earn enough to bring the rest of their family over to join them. They washed, and they talked, and reminisced and dreamt of better things to come. Silence fell eventually, and the sadness which lingered in the air seemed tangible. They wiped their tears away, and rolled into bed, in an effort to sleep off their problems. To my horror, as I gazed into the darkness, I saw that apart from the men sleeping on the bunks, others lay wrapped up in whatever they could find, between the chalk marks on the floor. I had thought that the chalk marks were to distinguish the boundaries between the bunks. Little did I realise that they also were sleeping places. This was home from home. Lying on that sofa, after travelling for fourteen days without a decent night's sleep and after a long day, I was more than ready for sleep. But I lay awake, and thought, "Is this the London I read about? Is this what London is all about?" Was this is a dream or reality – it was more like a nightmare. As the night wind whistled through the crackling windows and the missing window-panes covered with cardboard, my last conscious thought was that God who calls will care. I must have drifted off whilst praying into a deep sleep. I awoke next morning to find the room almost empty, the others already gone. I found a toilet and hand-basin in a cubicle which felt like an ice-box. No hot water, no soap, no towel. I managed the best I could, and later I ventured out into the streets, and prayed as I walked along the Euston Road shaking from head to toes with cold.

I walked up and down for two hours or more, choosing the back streets in order not to attract attention, just weeping and praying. I cried out to God to show me what he wanted me to do. Eventually, I reasoned that as God had called me here to be a missionary, I must be obedient to the heavenly vision. There was no better time to start than now. So, I began stopping people in the street and telling them about Jesus. At first, I thought that everyone would be glad to hear; after all, this was 'Christian England'; but I was soon made to see my mistake. People just did not want to know. I did not realise that in London you do not speak to people unless you are first introduced. There was a certain sterilised coldness which left one in no doubt that they did not wish their privacy to be intruded upon.

During that day, I thought I would find out what my £10 could buy. So I went into an Army Store, and after looking around I found a lovely warm RAF coat which just suited my pocket and with a couple of pounds to spare. That coat became my companion for a long time, shielding my body and warming me during those first cold months in Great Britain. I found a Salvation Army hostel where I rented a bed for my second night. After searching around, I heard of a group of people who engaged in street evangelism. I sought them out eventually, and applied to join. They were located in Barnet at the time. This was during the first week after my arrival. I landed on their doorstep early in the morning. Coming from a small country sugar plantation and also from a community which was more like an extended family, I did not know that you should not call unless you have made an appointment. To make matters worse, I stood there with my suitcase. I hate to think now what they must have thought when they answered the door and found me standing there. Oh, I was so naive. I thought that these were my brothers and sisters as they were missionaries, so naturally I must find my own family. Not knowing who I was or where I had come from they were kind enough to receive me, even though reluctantly.

While in this group, I learnt many precious lessons, both practical and spiritual. It was here that I learnt how to eat with a knife and fork. I could not believe my eyes, you could actually balance green peas on the back of a fork, lift them from a plate and successfully negotiate the flight to your mouth without an accident. After many trial runs, I acquired the skill. Here also I learnt how to do my washing. It is very different to the way we did it at home, and so is the way of preparing meals. I had never seen a gas cooker before – we used to cook on open fires. I shall ever remain grateful to Mrs. Smythe, who made it a mission of love to take an untrained, uncouth, semi-civilised country boy and patiently to instruct him in the finer points of life in England. It was here also, during the Bible study times, that my eyes were opened to many foundational truths which I knew by experience, but for which I had no theological explanation. These were the first people to give me the biblical basis for what I believed. It was here, too, that I first enjoyed fellowship with white, English Christians. I was having great fun. It was great to belong to a community of believers who were active in the town.

A dear friend who used to visit the group regularly belonged to an evangelical church. Dick invited me, and I gladly went with him. I felt at home because I was with my brothers and sisters in Christ. Could anything be more heavenly? There could not be any greater bond than fellowship with the family of God. I was soon to be disillusioned. After three visits, my friend and I were met at the door and told that they would be very pleased if I would never return to their meetings. Why? I was upsetting the believers. I asked why – had I done something wrong? "No, no, no", he said, very politely, and more than a little embarrassed. However, he stressed the point that much as he did not like to say it, he would be very glad if my friend Dick did not bring me again to their meetings. I could see the embarrassment on Dick's face. He was about to enter into an argument with the elder, but I persuaded him that it was all right with me, he needn't be hurt on my account. So we both went away, with tears in our eyes. To think that this could happen in a Christian, evangelical meeting. It was simply incredible, mind-boggling. Surely loving Jesus should mean accepting your brother whatever his colour or culture. My first taste of fellowship with white, evangelical English Christians left me bewildered and perplexed. It did not fall into my concept of New Testament Christianity. My friend Dick was a great source of support and strength. He was white and genuine. I was black: different and maybe in some ways rather backward, but he accepted me and treated me as an equal although in many ways he was so much more advanced than I.

I continued with this group in Barnet for six months and have many lovely memories which I shall always treasure. The prayer times, the study of the Word, the street evangelism, the adventures of faith, the bold and daring approach to witnessing in buses, tubes, and market-places. Once we were sent out on a mission. I had enough money to get there, but no money for the return journey. Mission completed, all my colleagues made their different ways home. I stood there not wanting to burden anyone. I prayed for help. "Go and join the queue to purchase your ticket." I simply obeyed. The queue was long, so I had time to build up my courage. With each disappearing person ahead of me, I rehearsed my lines. As it got shorter, I felt a lump in my throat. When there were only five people left, I knew it; I was panicking. I was too embarrassed to hop out of the line. Then it was down to three. By this time I was wishing that no-one knew I existed. Just then, someone rushed out of the crowd towards me, pressed something into my hand and disappeared. No, it was not an angel. This was a real person, but I cannot tell you who it was. I looked down in my hand – just enough for my fare back to Barnet.

One dull rainy Saturday afternoon, we were on the

escalator at Charing Cross singing "My Lord knows the way through the wilderness..." Very unorthodox. Heads turned and faces showing distinct disapproval stared at us. But a man in his late thirties was on his way to commit suicide. He was at the end of his tether. A proper, distinguished looking English gentleman, he wore a pin-striped suit, a bowler hat, and carried an umbrella. He listened to us, and was touched. He followed us into the train and one of our number witnessed to him. He accepted the Lord, his life turned completely round, and as I understand it, he served with distinction in a Christian society until his death just a few years ago. There was much joy and rejoicing that night. They were a truly super bunch.

In the early summer of 1956, a group of us was at Hyde Park Corner singing and testifying to great effect. Afterwards we broke up and spoke to individuals. I did not realise that the others had left. I was caught up with the crowd. I preached and shouted loud the Gospel, my theme, "Jesus, the only answer". The crowd heckled, pushed and jeered. Some cast cigarette ends. I was horrified at the blasphemous statements they hurled back at me. It was a horrific scene but I preached on, and finally prayed for one person to accept the Lord. I did not know that a group of Swedish young people under the leadership of two pastors was standing at the edge of the crowd, observing the whole scene. They waited until I had finished praying and was leaving, then they approached me and introduced themselves. We had an unforgettable time of prayer and fellowship. They enquired who I was, where I came from and what I was doing in Britain. They had a good laugh when I told them I was a missionary, and asked me about my conversion and subsequent events. As we parted, they gave me a gift of some money and a piece of paper with an invitation to visit them in Sweden. Hilding Fagerberg, a real big man in more ways than one, crushed me in a great big hug and repeated, "Come to Sweden."

"If it is the will of God, then..." I replied.

Precious memories, too numerous to report here, but they linger.

One Saturday in September the leader of the group summoned me to his office. He was a six-footer, always neatly dressed. He carried himself with a princely dignity. When he first accepted me, he treated me with much kindness, and in a way was like a real father to me. I was still only nineteen. He was a very good teacher and pastored me well. I had grown to esteem and love him; I felt secure with him.

As I entered the room, he beckoned me to sit down. Although he did not extend the usual warm cordiality, I did not suspect what was to follow, and prepared myself for one of his pastoral sessions. Then the unexpected happened. "I'm sorry Philip, but I can't keep you here any longer."

"Why?" I enquired in half-choked and subdued voice.

"Oh, you have deceived us long enough. I'm sorry I did not find you out from the very beginning. But now I know that you do not have any calling on your life. You will never make it as a missionary. The real reason that you are here is to get free food and board," he replied determinedly. Nothing could have shocked me more than that, because all the time it had seemed that God had joined me to this group of people, and I had come to love them very much. They had accepted me, and I thought they were training and moulding me in order that I might come into the full realisation of the calling that God had given to me. What could I say? I couldn't argue; how could I prove to him that I had a calling from God? In vain, I tried to say a few words, to explain my position and my desire to serve God. I was met with a very cold and calculated rebuff: "Get out. I don't want to see you here by six o'clock." There was no enquiry or explanation. I was unilaterally dismissed. In fact, one of my brother workers had fabricated tales against me which were quite unfounded, for reasons of his own. This other worker was white. He had very serious character problems, a violent temper and homosexual tendencies. For three months I sought to be a friend, to counsel him, pray for him and minister to him. Then this! Unfortunately the leader accepted his stories at face value and did not think to ask any questions.

His words struck a deep blow. I felt a sinking, sickening sensation. I reached into my pocket, and I remember feeling the edges of three pennies. Three pennies . . . no shelter, no friends, no contacts, just three sad-looking pennies. I felt all alone. I rose up, a little weak at the knees, shocked by what I had just heard. I was hurting.

The thought that I was just scrounging filled me with horror, I had always been poor, but my parents believed in the dignity of work. I considered seeking employment, or pursuing my life-long ambition to become a doctor. The last thing I wanted to do was to live on the charity of others and be regarded as a parasite feeding on their backs. I would sweep the streets, clean the toilets, do anything rather than live with this sense of indignity. Yet I felt a strong pull to be true to my calling. It would have been easier to cast off the invisible constraints that such a sense of vocation brings and follow my natural inclinations to study medicine, but there was never any thought of going back on Jesus. I was shaken, but still wanted to serve the Lord and my fellow man. However these men of God, leaders, felt I was not a missionary. My confidence was undermined. I was filled with doubts about the validity of my call. I questioned again and again, was I mistaken, even deceived? What could I do in this mighty metropolis? Maybe God did not really call me after all. The conflict now raged within me between calling and career. I was caught on the horns of a serious dilemma ... I was at a crossroads.

As I lifted my heart God-ward, I was transported back in time to a small village on the east bank of the Essequibo, where I had encountered God. It was there that I first heard his call to become a missionary. I remembered how I struggled with that call for three long months, the way God dealt with me until I surrendered and submitted to his will, and the peace that flooded my heart when I said an unequivocal 'yes'. The miraculous provision of the ticket and all that followed – could it all be a mistake? After all, I was only a young Christian. This brother and his team were far more experienced and mature. They should know. I knew very little about 'Divine guidance'. I felt as if the ground had been taken from beneath my feet: doubts assailing, knees trembling, energy draining, but the heart still clinging to God, praying. An eternity must have been pressed into those few fleeting moments as I contemplated my situation. Suddenly, unmistakably, that same voice which first said: "Follow me" spoke tender reassurances. It was warm, comforting and healing. Once again my heavenly Father met me and confirmed my calling. With new confidence I rose up, determined that man had not called me; God had. If he had, then I was ultimately accountable to him. My response to such love and authority could only be, "where you lead, I will follow – lead on light, lead on."

I bade farewell to the group who had been my family for six months. I have not seen most of them again. I pulled on my faithful RAF coat and stepped out of the front door into nowhere, fully convinced that I was in the will of God. I had no clue as to what the future held, no idea what was ahead. I only knew that you cannot lose if you follow the Lamb. I could only step forward in faith.

CHAPTER SIX

I come to Brixton

I started walking in the general direction of central London. The sun was shining, a beautiful day, but already it was growing cold. I walked a little and also hitched a ride here and there. "Where are you going?" I would ask people who offered me a lift. I felt I was seeking an unknown land and destiny.

Some well-meaning friends in Potters Bar had suggested that it might be the best thing for me to head for Brixton, because they understood that it was the one place in London where blacks congregated and settled. I pondered the suggestion. The idea did not really interest me. It sounded like 'go find your own kind'. It had racial undertones. Inherent in the suggestion was segregation with all its ugly consequences. The spectre of conflict and tension between races, black and white, loomed large on the distant horizon, like a gigantic evil omen; but the closer I got to the centre of London, the more intense the pressure became to make a decision. I had no alternatives, no other options open to me. So, I reckoned that maybe the Lord had something or someone there, and to Brixton I went.

It was in late October 1956 that I made my entry into Brixton town. It was three in the afternoon, and the weather had changed by now. It is really amazing that at any given time of year one can experience almost four seasons in the same day. Now the skies were overcast, dark, heavy and threatening a rain or sleet shower. It grew considerably colder. There I was, a diminutive figure standing right in the middle of Brixton at the junction of Atlantic Road and Coldharbour Lane, under the railway bridge. I surveyed the scene, the famous arcade and market stalls stretched in an unending arrangement of all sorts of exotic foods alongside the traditional British vegetables and fruits. Many people mingled with the buses, cars and vans in the narrow streets, clutching shopping bags, moving in and out of the network of arcades. The pub on the corner was crowded, men and women filing in and out of its large brown doors. Some of them negotiated their way among the crowds with a distinctly unsteady gait – inebriated, I supposed.

Since my arrival at Victoria I had not seen so many people of my own colour in one place. There were men and women, many ill-clad for the climate. Some had obtained heavy overcoats, others looked obviously cold, or just lost and bewildered. Disillusionment was written indelibly on many faces. I stood there, tapping my feet and rubbing my hands to keep the circulation going. The scene was beginning to affect me as I looked and observed. Here were thousands of people far away from their natural habitat, willing to endure conditions of hardship in order to make something of their lives and to create a better brighter future for their children. In spite of the intermingling, somehow there was no real sense of integration; they did not seem to belong. A people uprooted: a migrant minority, searching for a place in the sun, a home in a foreign country, for a future. The last verses of the ninth chapter of Matthew's Gospel came vividly into focus in my mind, where the Lord sees the people as sheep without a shepherd, and calls for labourers in his harvest. These people were like sheep distressed, weary and downcast and without a shepherd.

"Is there a harvest in that multitude?" I questioned.

"Can I be a shepherd to them?" I muttered with some doubt.

"Is it possible that this is my first mission field?" I contemplated.

I must have been there for more than an hour, just observing the situation. My heart was melted and I felt compassion flowing out of me, so that I wanted to touch the people with love, God's love. Hot tears bathed my tired face. I knew that my Father was waiting for a response.

"Yes, Lord, I will. How, I do not know, but with your help, I will." In that open street corner, with the occasional rumble of trains just above my head, I made a commitment and dedication to serve the people here in Brixton as the Lord would enable and provide.

It was getting darker, night was already approaching, the street lights came on and it was raining now. I was hungry and wishing desperately that I could sit down in a warm dry place. I moved towards Somerleyton Road and looked up through the constant drizzle, as if to touch my Father beyond the thick dark clouds, and prayed: "Lord, I need a room to live in, and food."

I was sure God had it all worked out. In my simple conversational manner I said, "Could you direct me to the house and the people you have prepared." I would come to a junction and wait for an inner prompting, whether to turn left or right. It is amazing, I actually received instructions through a series of such inner promptings: 'Turn right', 'Go across', 'Turn left', and so on. Eventually I felt the Holy Spirit say "Stop." It was number 53 Barrington Road.

"Go up the steps and knock," I was prompted. So I did. A small neatly dressed and energetic-looking white woman with a delightful smile came to the door. I explained that I was looking for a room to rent. "That's strange," she exclaimed. "Only a few days ago, I began praying that God would bring me the right tenant for this room, which I have not let out for many years. Who are you?" I told her that I was a Christian, that God had guided me to the Brixton area to be a missionary. She looked at me, somewhat astonished, not really sure what to believe or think. A little man not even a hundred pounds in weight, suddenly at her door-step saying he wants to be a missionary to England. A black man in a white country – a heathen man in a Christian country; what could this mean?

"Come back in a few hours," she said, "and I will give you my decision." I wandered around the streets, thinking and praying.

"God, if that place is for me, speak to that landlady. If it isn't, I don't want it." I said this, fully knowing that it was late evening and it was cold and raining. I needed a place to sleep that night. I didn't feel like spending another night in another coal shed, or sitting on some cold bench, or parked in a shop window. I would really welcome a decent room in which to lay my weary head. I knocked at the door again, half trembling, expecting the worst; half believing, expecting her to say yes. You know, those mixed emotions that you go through on occasions when you are in a crisis. Anyway, I turned up at the appointed hour, quite soaked by this time, and knocked and waited. She opened the door.

"So," she said, "I must be half crazy, but I can't get away from the feeling that God wants me to give you that room. Come inside, and have a hot cup of tea, and then I'll show it to you. Fifteen shillings per week." Welcome words of comfort and relief; music to my ears. So she showed me into the living room, and after a cup of tea she took me into the room. She was so kind. She gave me linen for the bed and put a hot water bottle in it and a heater in the room. Exhausted, I rolled into a nice warm bed and did not remember any more until the morning light, streaming through the curtains, woke me up.

That basement room became my sanctuary. For many months I not only ate and slept there, but that was where I met God. Over and over again, in the late hours of the night, the early hours of the morning, God came down and spoke with me and taught me things from the Bible that I had never heard before: things that I did not know at the time but upon which my whole future ministry would be built. Later on, I discovered that God was saying the same radical, revolutionary things to many men of God throughout the country at that time: things concerning the Church, things concerning the Holy Spirit and the gifts of the Spirit, things concerning eldership, and many other truths which are now so popular. God was teaching me in his own way in that humble basement room, my own private meeting place with God. I dubbed it the Sanctuary.

During my time there, some very significant things happened. For one thing, God miraculously provided that fifteen shillings every week. I would wend my way up to the third floor to Alice and Betty with a smile on my face – no need to be ashamed. As Christian women, they understood that every time I took that fifteen shillings, they were witnessing God's faithfulness to me. It was always followed by a time of prayer and a cup of tea. I cherished those moments of fellowship, around their tea table. Once, I had no food for three days. I was really getting hungry by the end of the second day. In my need I cried to God, "Please provide me with some food, and some money for my rent." The miraculous happened. I expected that God would send me the money through the mail-box or in some other way, but instead he used Mrs. Denbow, who was living on the ground floor.

She cried out at the top of her voice: "Philip, can you do me a favour?"

"Sure," I said, "What is it?"

"Oh," she said, "I've peeled some extra potatoes

today. There's no way we could use them all. Would you feel insulted if I offered you a few of them – I'd cook them. By the way, rather than just give you potatoes, I've extra greens and a piece of meat if you don't mind." What could I say but thank you, Jesus! Without knowing whether it was a conscious mistake or not, God had used her to provide a meal for a son of his who was very hungry that day.

That basement room became my base. After my morning duties and prayers I would pack my brief-case with Billy Graham tracts and New Testaments and any other literature I could find and venture into the streets of Brixton. I preached in Woolworths, in pubs (especially the Prince of Wales) and on the buses. I knocked on doors from Clapham to Camberwell, from Kennington to Streatham Hill. I stood often in the open air and market place, giving out tracts on the streets and making contacts with many. 'God's plan of Salvation' and 'Four things God wants you to know' were the two leaflets I used most.

So my days were made up of eight to ten hours of witnessing on the streets, preaching in the open air, and generally making myself a nuisance to the Devil, and maybe to a few people as well. Often the police would stop me and ask where I got my authority to do this. I would promptly point them to John Chapter 15, verse 16 which says, "You have not chosen me, but I have chosen you, that you should go, and bring forth fruit." Some policemen were amused, others stopped and listened as I witnessed to them; others were disgusted, but felt that I wasn't doing much harm to anybody, so they let me go. As a result of this simple, and sometimes not very wise witnessing, people began to accept Christ.

Another important thing happened while I was in Brixton, which played a significant part in the direction my life would take later. In December 1956 God met me, and showed me a vision of the West Indies and

Guyana – a vision which I shall describe more fully later – in which certain places stood out as strategic areas in which he wanted to plant churches; places from which his word would spread. I could not see how this could ever be, but I hid it deep in my heart and continued to pray. As I prayed and read, and waited in my Father's presence in my basement room at number 53 Barrington Road, my life was transformed and enriched. I will always cherish the moments of fellowship, my miraculous provision for rent and food, and most of all, the times alone with my Father, my Lord, and the Holy Spirit, in my own private little sanctuary there.

CHAPTER SEVEN

Sheep needing a shepherd

Being a missionary in Brixton was exciting and challenging. The area was definitely needy. There were thousands of people needing help – homeless, discouraged, unemployed, disillusioned people: people whose dreams were shattered, who could not cope with the cold weather, who were separated from family and friends. They had started to arrive during the war, recruited as soldiers to fight for their king and country. Later, they were invited to take up certain jobs in hospitals, factories and transport services, especially in the post-war years, the early fifties. They were encouraged to come because they were filling many jobs that others would not consider taking at that time, so they fulfilled a vital function in the reconstruction of the economy and in the rebuilding programme after the war. By the mid-fifties, families began joining their loved ones, and others came seeking education or because of the scarcity of job opportunities in the West Indies. Naturally they had looked to their mother country for help in their hour of need and depression, but now there was not always work for all these people, and life was difficult for them in many ways.

Some were drawn into the drug scene in the Somerleyton Road area. Young women were deceived by unscrupulous men who took advantage of their plight, exploited them and then ditched them. This was the field where I must labour. I worked on the principle that I should put in at least eight hours a day in direct evangelism, convinced that Christians should be industrious and diligent in all they do. Time management and stewardship were essential to the success of any effort. To reap, I must sow; to have reward, I must invest. I sought to set priorities and stick to them. I knocked systematically on doors. Generally I met with a hostile reception, but some people were interested. At street corners, and wherever people were to be found I lifted up my voice and preached as loudly as I could above the noise of the traffic, proclaiming Jesus, the friend and Saviour of all mankind.

At first, no-one took very much notice, but after a few weeks, people realised that I was not going away. Some people accepted Christ as Saviour and Lord, while others attempted to run me off the streets. Through my work in the streets and market-places, I also came into contact with people who were Christians before they came to Britain. They were attracted either by my preaching or the leaflets. They would come up and introduce themselves in tears, telling me how they were starved for real Christian warmth and fellowship. Some of them had been in the country for a couple of years, but had found no place where they could express their worship freely, and feel at home. Many of them related unpleasant incidents they had suffered. They were cold-shouldered when they went to churches or straight-forwardly asked not to return as they were an embarrassment to the other members of the congregation. People actually said that when they entered certain buildings for worship and sat down, some worshippers would either get up and move down the bench, or move to another row. At the end of the meeting, the pastor saying goodbye to everyone at the door would turn his back on them, as if to pretend they did not exist. And these were the same people who had sent missionaries out to them! It was bewildering and perplexing, to say the least. If they were good enough to belong to the same denomination in the West Indies, why were they not good enough to belong here? A brother told me that a Bishop actually told him that he could not have the use of a building, even though they had no other use for it. This building was closed, redundant, but God's people could not use it. The people under the Bishop's care would be very upset. It was heart-rending. These stories I simply would not have believed, but having suffered something similar myself, I realised that they were true and not just lame excuses or malicious gossip.

Apart from the snobbery and rejection which West Indians were experiencing, they also felt estranged and alienated from the style of worship. The hymns and the liturgy were often almost the same as they were used to, but the atmosphere was dull, the singing dry with almost no heart in the songs, the preaching cold and calculated. They felt that the church worship was uninviting and unattractive, especially when it seemed so irrelevant to their need and to the deepseated questions which they faced. The situation was not helped either by the small attendance in many churches. Can you imagine their consternation when they walked into a gloomy building that could seat four hundred, to find thirty or forty? They came in with high expectations and went out not only deflated but confused. Why do the whites not go to church, they would ask themselves. This was a shock – a definite culture-shock. They felt hurt, and became very suspicious, fearing rejection. Some of them vowed that if this was what Jesus and Christianity was all about, they wanted no part in it.

Had it been a deliberate plan to deceive us in order to rule and exploit us? They became conscious of discrimination, racial prejudice, of being second class citizens, unwanted and not respected. These ideas were watered and the concepts further fortified by ugly experiences of discrimination in the factories, schools, offices, hospitals and in job- and house-hunting. To add insult to injury, they were constantly told that they were no good – like Ron, a young man who lives in East London who when he was at school sat an exam with a group of white children. At the end the teacher called him and demanded that he reveal the source from which he had copied the work. She just could not accept that a black boy could produce such a good paper. When he protested his innocence, she insisted that he was lying and penalised him. He felt so embarrassed in front of his class-mates, and so undervalued. The thought that he was not good enough or equal has never left him. Now that he has accepted Christ, we are seeking to lift him out of his misery.

Many have never gone back to church to this day. Their faith was undermined, wrecked and overthrown. They gave up Jesus, the Bible and the Church. They turned to other things and to other ideologies to fill the vacuum created by the lack of the friendship and fellowship to which they were accustomed in the West Indies. I thought long and hard about this situation and prayed for guidance: "Lord, show me what to do. There are many bleeding, wounded, hurt sheep out there, and they are left as prey to the devil."

I took names and addresses of those who accepted Christ, those who expressed an interest, and those who were seeking for fellowship. In the evenings, I would meet them in their homes. Some evenings, I would visit as many as seven homes, spending time with them, counselling them, listening to their problems and praying with them. It was during this period, when there was a great influx of immigrants, that the housing situation became acute. White landlords would bluntly turn away tenants simply because they were black. They would advertise in shop windows, but if a black person turned up, he would be told that there was no vacancy. Some white person would come later on, and would get it. There were some landlords who would rather not rent their flat out, than have a black tenant.

The more expensive flats and houses that were available were above the means of the newcomers. Those who came a few years earlier and had been able to buy property took advantage of the situation to make some money, and at the same time to help the people from their own country, and prevent them having to sleep on the streets. They divided up their dwelling houses into rooms to let. They shared the bathroom, and installed as many as three stoves in the kitchen, each with its own coin-operated meter. Each double room would be let to a family, while singles had the box-rooms. There could be up to six different families, twenty people in the one house. It has to be said that the landlords did not really look after their properties, and the houses were often in a very poor state of repair – wall-paper torn, rattling windows with missing panes. There was no proper heating, and the overcrowding definitely affected the inhabitants' health. Nevertheless, the black landlords provided an invaluable service to the new immigrants. They did not select their tenants, and often would wait for the rent until the tenant could find a job. I was amazed to see the people scrub and clean, and decorate run-down places and turn their room into a home. They made a home out of a room – a home away from home. Each room would have a bed, a wardrobe, a dining table, a couple of chairs, boxes and suitcases under the bed and on top of the wardrobe. There would be a baby-cot in the corner; it was congested, yet they were thankful to have a place to shelter.

The camaraderie, the encouragement and support that the inmates would give to one another was certainly a major factor in keeping many from going insane and preventing them from suffering a nervous breakdown. It meant too that each house became a mission field. There was a potential congregation in every house. I sought to use one contact in a house as a means of reaching the others. As many as twelve, sometimes fifteen people would gather together in one room, singing, praying and studying the word. I called it 'the church in the home'.

Around this same time, I heard that there was another brother who was working amongst the immigrant population in the Brixton area. A few months earlier, he had successfully conducted a tent-crusade on a bombed-out site, right in the middle of Somerleyton Road. I heard many good things of him and the work he was doing, and so I sought him out. It was love at first sight. We decided that we should work together, not separately. We combined our gifts and meagre resources and began to work together as a team. This was Ken. He had been converted through the ministry of a Baptist preacher in Jamaica. He came to the UK and worked in a metal-work factory, but soon received the call to become an evangelist, and had stepped out in faith in obedience to this call. He was an inch or two taller than I was, a lot more mature, wiser and more able in many ways than I was, married to an English woman who stood by his side. Joan was a real encourager, not only to Ken, but also to me. She worked long, hard hours to care for their children, as well as to do all the secretarial work involved in our young missionary enterprise. Ken had already established a country-wide preaching circuit, but every week he found time to come from Dorking where he lived and spend a couple of days working with me on the streets and in the market places of Brixton.

As a result of our ministry, the number of people who now looked to us for help, for ministry, and who regarded us as their pastors, was increasing. We encouraged them to accompany us to the existing

churches in the area, but for the reasons already
described, they did not feel at home. Even in the more
lively churches, the people made no attempt to involve
us in the life and fabric of the family. We could attend
the meetings, but could not participate in leadership.
We felt like outsiders, visitors, and not part of the family.
We had very little option therefore than to gather the
fruits of our outdoor and door-to-door ministry, and
provide for them some sort of church life. It was never
our original intention. We felt from the beginning that
having contacted and helped them initially on the street
and in their homes, we should feed them back into the
mainstream of the church. Unfortunately, this was
never to be. So, we looked around Brixton for a suitable
place where we could gather those who were interested.
This was almost an impossibility, but we found a
gentleman, a backslidden Christian from Jamaica, who
had lived in this country for a few years. He had a
tailor's shop in a basement room which could
accommodate fifty people. We pleaded with this tailor
to allow us to use his shop for our meetings. This kind
gentleman would push his machines away in one corner,
and pack up his materials in a cupboard to make space
for us every Sunday night.

I waited with baited breath that first Sunday – I was
not sure whether anyone would turn up. This was new
ground, new experience for me, still only nineteen years
old. On the appointed hour, there was one, then two – I
felt relieved. It would not just be the tailor and me.
About fifteen minutes after the hour, we were a good
dozen. By half past, the room was nearly full. We sang
lustily the old gospel hymns and lively choruses: 'Jesus
set me free one day...' and so on. The sound filled the
night air outside. People drawn by the sound began to
flock around that little basement. I was taken by
complete surprise. The basement became crowded
inside and out.

"O Lord they are hungry. They want you. Thank you

Lord." I praised him as they pressed into every available space and strained their ears to hear. Often the proceedings were interrupted by a shout of "Praise the Lord, Amen Brother, O thank you Jesus. Glory!" Some wept openly, unashamedly admitting their loneliness and lack of fellowship, and even confessed that they were growing cold and drifting away from the Lord. Week after week we preached, ministered, prayed for the sick and for people to find jobs. People who were lonely, hopeless, heavy, sad, unemployed, we faithfully sought to support through prayer and encouragement. Week by week they returned with stories of victory. God answered their prayers: their bills were paid, jobs were provided, the sick were healed, lives were changing. People who were caught up in the net of the seamier side of London life, suddenly began to turn to Christ and to God. We saw many miracles down in that basement; many were challenged and changed and given new hope. Ken and I continued ministering during the week in different homes which now were spread over other areas as well as Brixton: Streatham, Camberwell, Thornton Heath, Dalston, Croydon, Norwood, Hackney and Tottenham, to name but a few.

We met a lady in Brixton Road who wept unashamedly outside the Lambeth Town Hall. In between sobs, she related that she was a Christian from Jamaica who upon arrival in this country had fallen on hard times. With no job, no friends, and no place to live, she met a fellow who lured and enticed her by promising her the world. She fell both for him and for his offer to share his life. When she became pregnant, everything changed. He left her, and simply disappeared without trace. Now she was landed with a baby, had to pay rent, and could not find work. She was cold and she looked so weak and frail. Her eyes sunk deep in their sockets mirrored the hurt and brokenness in her spirit, her beautiful ebony face was marred by the stress and strain of the past year. As we listened our hearts were touched, tears now flowing freely from us as well. We reassured her of God's love and care. All was not lost. Jesus could give her a new beginning. We bowed our heads together in the stream of unconscious passers-by and the constant flow of traffic, and all prayed fervently. She felt relieved. We parted with a promise to visit her.

Next day I called at number 9 Wiltshire Road where she lived. The door was open. I entered and called – no response. The entrance and passage-way were bare, the walls and ceiling dull and gloomy. Obviously no-one had repaired or decorated the place for ages. I climbed up the bare wooden stairs with paint peeling off and hanging on the sides. Hearing the faint sound of crying, I followed the sound and quietly knocked. Slowly the door opened. There she was, her eyes still wet with her tears. She invited me in and explained that she was praying that the Lord would send her help and give her a new start. The room was neat although cramped. Baby lay wrapped up on the bed, face flushed and running a temperature. I went out and bought her some coal, some groceries, vegetables and something from Boots for the baby. She lit a fire and set about preparing something to eat while I washed the baby's nappies and swept out the passage way and stairs. After prayer, I departed. She felt better with each visit. Once when I came, she had gathered three others in her little room. It was only about ten feet by twelve, and it was bedroom, kitchen and dining room for her and the baby. We sat on the bed and on the two chairs. You could hardly turn round in that room, but it was her home. I preached to three people as though they were three hundred.

We did not know that in the adjoining room there was a gentleman who was listening and who felt naked and exposed by the things I was saying. He concluded that the lady must have informed me about him, that I was now indirectly seeking to preach to him and to tell his story to the people gathered there. He felt embarrassed and became very angry. The Holy Spirit was really seeking to draw this man to himself, but instead of responding to God he became incensed. Tall, burly and muscular, he came out of his room and ordered me never to come back or else he would not be responsible for the consequences. He was mad. I returned the following week, as planned. He had anticipated that his threat would not keep me away, so he and his soldier son were locked up in their room waiting to see if I would turn up. As soon as I entered the room, I felt rather restrained. I sat down and allowed the conversation to drift back and forth. There was no real urge to preach or to say anything. Eventually, I suggested that we pray. As we were praying, the door burst open and in walked a strong, tall handsome man. I knew instinctively that he was no friend. He looked fierce and almost frightening. He came in and sat down. We sat in silence for some time, and I felt that it was time to go. As I reached for the door and began to leave, he spoke up and said:

"Who are you? What is in you?"

"Oh, I'm just an ordinary Christian," I replied.

"Well, there's something about you I don't understand," he carried on in a subdued tone.

"Really?" I said.

"Well," he continued, "did you know that I came here to throw you out of the window?" whereupon he revealed a knife. It suddenly dawned on me that we were on the third floor. It was a long drop for flesh to touch concrete, I thought.

Then he continued: "But mister, whoever you are, please pray for me, because when I entered the room, my arms were paralysed, and I still can't move them properly. Would you pray for me?"

Tears filled my eyes as I realised that God had once again spared my life. "God, this young man really needs you." I felt a deep compassion and prayed for him. He regained the use of his limbs, and we parted on the best of terms. Whenever he was home, he would look me up, and we became real friends. As a result, I had free access to that home, and several people in it received Jesus.

CHAPTER EIGHT

Set-backs and harvest

Through the 'churches in the home', witnessing on the streets and the Sunday evening meetings, the number of believers grew. The calls for pastoral care increased and so also the demands on our time. Every day we found more needy people in other areas; with every passing week new challenges presented themselves. Every month too, new recruits for jobs arrived from the different islands of the Caribbean. With every new wave the problem of housing became more acute. With our meagre resources already stretched to breaking point, we had to choose to limit what we did or to expand our operation to cope with the growing need. The question was, how could we cope with more? There are only twenty-four hours in one day.

There is one way to do it, and the Bible shows us what that is: reproduce, train up others, as Paul trained Timothy. At last therefore we decided to give extra, deeper teaching to equip others to help us in the task of evangelism and social care. One Mr. Leslie who owned a large house with three floors and a basement in Somerleyton Road loaned us the basement, free of charge, in which to conduct evening classes. Mr. Leslie was one of those West Indians who had chosen to settle in England after fighting in the war, and to contribute to post-war rebuilding. Those teaching sessions in his house were some of the loveliest times we ever had. We were just ten in the beginning, then fifteen, then twenty.

Eventually thirty eager people packed into that room. The curriculum was simple and handled such subjects as the doctrine of God, the person of Jesus, evangelism, how to be a soul-winner, and an in-depth study of the Books of Romans and Acts. The evening was divided into three fifty-minute sessions. There was an eagerness, a hunger in those who came, that made them a real joy to teach. Many of them were not particularly gifted academically but week after week we saw lives changing and people becoming more enlightened. They were blessed and strengthened to cope with the temptations and testings of a completely different culture and environment. They were equipped and made bold to witness to their faith. We took them out on Sunday afternoons to work with us on the streets.

It was in this mid-week training and Bible-study meeting that I met Eva Carr, a young Jamaican who had come to this country to do nursing. She was at Netherne Hospital in Coulsdon, Surrey, and each week she travelled up to join us. She witnessed to another Jamaican girl also doing nursing at the same hospital whose name was Muriel Inez Leonara LeMonte. They were both part of the recruitment programme conducted in the colonies after the war. Through Eva's faithful witnessing Muriel accepted Christ one night in their hostel room. This young lady was constantly depressed and filled with fears, and had some deep personal problems. Brought up by her grandmother in a religious environment, she had always been a church-goer and had been very involved in the activities of the church in Jamaica. She was christened, confirmed, sang in the choir, attended church regularly, but did not have a born-again experience of Christ until that night when she accepted him through Eva's faithful witness. Muriel later explained that it was not just her witnessing, but the beauty of the life of her friend Eva that had attracted her. She was different – happy and

always smiling. After the classes, Eva went back to
Coulsdon and related to Muriel the blessings she had
received from the Bible studies, adding, "One night you
must come and meet this small dynamic man with the
biggest voice I have ever heard." As I heard afterwards,
this throw-away comment provoked hilarious laughter,
and then was dismissed for the time being.

The Sunday evening meetings and the outdoor
ministry were bearing fruit. Now we had a new
problem: we had to consider baptising those who
accepted Christ. By this time we were beginning to come
into contact with other churches in the area. Most of
them were sceptical about what we were doing in spite
of the efforts we made to work together, but a couple of
pastors encouraged us to continue the work. They were
helpful, they prayed with us, lectured in our classes and
counselled us a few times. They were from Gresham
Road and Stockwell Baptist churches. Stockwell Baptist
loaned us their baptistry, and we were able then to
organise our first baptismal service. Ten people were
baptised in 1957. We had a packed house for this
meeting. While I was leading the singing, I looked across
at the baptismal candidates and realised that there was
a young lady whom I did not recognise. She must be the
one Ken had prepared for the occasion. Then – horror of
horrors! Right in the middle of that meeting charged
with a lovely sense of God's presence, I found myself
thinking: "There's your wife!" You can imagine the
violent reaction within me. I was now about twenty
years of age. I rebuked the Devil with all the strength I
could muster, without screaming out for others to hear. I
knew definitely that the Devil was tempting me. Right
in the middle of a meeting! A baptismal meeting! So the
thing was rebuked and dismissed. That was that, I
thought. That was the first time I saw Muriel.

My little basement in Barrington Road was a real
sanctuary for me, and my fellowship with Alice and

Betty, and with the Denbows who also lived there was a source of strength and encouragement. They were white, but they were kind and they accepted me as I was. They often prayed with Ken and me. Alice and Betty took me to their church and introduced me to their pastor. I faithfully went with them each Sunday morning for many months, and one day the pastor called me up and told me that Alice and Betty had requested that I give my testimony to the church.

"But," he said, "We'd like to find out something about you first." I thought that was fair enough. He was very impressed with my story and then he asked, "Where did you study? What degree do you have? What Bible school did you attend?" I wondered at the relevance of the inquiry.

"Unfortunately, I have not attended Bible school, and do not have a degree," I told him, somewhat mystified.

"I'm sorry, then I can't allow you to speak." Two things crossed my mind at this point. Firstly, that there were others who had given their testimony but did not hold degrees. Secondly, I wondered what this man would make of our Sunday evening meetings, which were far larger in numbers than the meetings in his chapel. I just thanked him politely and said nothing, but was left feeling that the Church in England was missing a golden opportunity: a mission field on its doorstep; the world in miniature on the streets of London; the far flung channels of the Empire flowing back. The various colours and diversity which enrich the Commonwealth were now right here on their doorstep and they did not really want to know. What a responsibility! What an opportunity – to trap this whole immigrant stream, to reach them with Christ's love, give them a home, evangelise them, train them, and possibly send them back to their own country, reversing the stream as it were, especially in the face of mission field after mission field being closed to western missionaries and to western methods. I felt very sad. An advantage was being surrendered. This opportunity once lost may never be regained.

I locked myself in my room and wept, not because I could not testify in the chapel, but because of the lack of vision and strategy of God's people. The sheer arrogance and pettiness of the situation was difficult to handle. I thanked God for Alice, Betty and Dick, the two pastors and other white Christians who were different. Nevertheless I could not disguise the hurt and pain I felt inside. Many questions lingered that demanded clarification. As I prayed, I felt that the Church in Britain should wake up and change its attitudes and its missionary concepts. It seemed that it was all right for the missionaries to go to so-called 'uncivilised savages' in India, Africa and the West Indies, to win us, plant churches and teach us to preach out there. Here it was not permissible. Something had to be wrong.

Just after my twentieth birthday, Ken arranged a little tour for me through some of the towns and villages of southern England. It was a great experience and widened my vision considerably. Upon my return, it was no longer possible for me to occupy my basement room, as Alice and Betty felt they had an obligation to a long-standing tenant in the house who needed it. They were very sad about it, but I understood the position, and agreed that it was only right that the other person should have my room. What else can a Christian do? It meant, however, that I was once again without shelter. I found a room a few streets away. It was not like the basement. It was scruffy but I was happy. Beggars can not be choosers. After the first week, the landlady called for her rent, which was payable a week in advance. Unfortunately, I only had the money in a postal order. The post office was closed. I pleaded with her to give me until next morning. She could not wait and demanded that I get out right there and then.

"Give me back the keys", she demanded. Nothing more to do. I asked Alice and Betty to keep my luggage for a few days without giving any explanation and went out into the night. I filled my RAF coat pockets with tracts and prepared myself for another night on the streets. I walked up and down Coldharbour Lane from Brixton Road to Loughborough Junction. Up and down, up and down, giving out the tracts, speaking to people. The hours to midnight passed rather quickly. I was busy. In the early hours of the morning, there were very few people around. I paused from time to time to rest my legs in a shop door, fearing that if I stayed too long, the police would question me. I kept moving, walking, resting and remembering the other nights I had spent out in the cold streets. I walked and prayed and even indulged in a praise game. With the left foot down I would say "Hallelujah!", right foot down, "Praise the Lord!" It served to keep me awake and not feeling too sorry for myself. About 2.30 a.m., something was beginning to happen. God was creating a whole new sense of tomorrow within me. Early morning. I began thinking it was time we moved to larger premises. We needed more rooms, not just a single room; a place where we could take the destitute and also accommodate one or two members attached to us in the team. They would live with us, be further discipled by us, and work with us. The night soon drifted to four o'clock in the morning, and between four and six, each hour felt like a whole night. At six in the morning, feeling sleepy and a little the worse for wear, I stopped in front of a shop window. There, displayed on a card, in not too legible writing, were the words: 'Four rooms to rent, six pounds a week.'

"This can't be true. Am I seeing right?" I wondered. Well, six pounds a week was a lot of money in those days.

I was able to muster £5 a week income and my faith was bigger than reality, so I made my way to 40 Overton Road. The time, 7 a.m. It was quiet and peaceful. Apart from the milkman going his rounds there was hardly any sign of life. A heavy mist caressed the rooftops. The occasional chirping of birds from the trees lining both sides of the road broke the stillness of the morning. I knocked somewhat timidly. An elderly white lady came to the door. She was surprised to see a young black man standing outside her door at that early hour. "What do you want?" she said. She sounded as if she had not long woken up.

"I saw your advertisement in a shop window in Coldharbour Lane, saying that you have rooms to let."

"Oh yes," she said. "But surely you are not thinking of renting them? How many do you want?" she asked with a puzzled expression.

"Is it possible for me to have all four?" I responded as though I was trying to reassure and convince myself.

"What would you do with four rooms?" she enquired in a kind and friendly manner. I explained my vision of the night before.

"Oh," she said, "I'm not too sure about that." I was not too sure myself but I spent some time showing her what my vision was, and what we were seeking to do in the district. She was not a Christian, and not particularly religious either.

"Oh, that should be all right then, but you must promise me one thing: No hanky-panky business in my house," she said firmly.

"Madam, we are Christians, there is no fear of that." I assured her that we would be well-behaved, that we were clean and above board.

Later that day, Ken and I put together enough to give her the first week's rent in advance. I hurried back to collect my luggage before Alice and Betty left for work. A couple of sisters and a brother from the Sunday night meeting helped Ken and me to give the place a good scrub and clean. Our new landlady was pleased and impressed. Our first centre for evangelism in the Brixton area! The base for the International Evangelical Fellowship as we were now called. One room for the sisters, two for the brothers on the top floor, and one all-purpose room. We were given a lovely table and a couple of beds. The work steadily grew and increased in membership. The Sunday night meetings were now taking place in the basement of Mr. Leslie's house in Somerleyton Road and we continued them there, but we started Bible classes in Overton Road.

One day we had an urgent call from one of our young converts who suffered from nervousness and depression. Misfortune had overtaken her, her cousin had been stabbed and was lying in hospital where doctors were fighting to save her life. She was just a hair's breadth between life and death. We rushed over to the hospital and prayed for the dying to live. There was not much else we could do. We tried to comfort the convert. The desperately ill girl hung in the balance for two days and then to the amazement of the doctors recovered enough to be discharged within a week. They both came to live with us in our new little centre, and both turned out to be pillars of the church.

A thirty-five-year-old man had nowhere to live. He walked the streets, destitute and abandoned. He had come to this country with high hopes, had searched in vain to find a room, and his money was now spent. We met him on the Brixton Road as we were witnessing one afternoon, a tall, strikingly handsome Jamaican, and prayed with him as he desired to accept the Lord. You could see the strain and distress on his face. I was glad that we were able to say to him, "Come and stay with us." He shared a room with the rest of us men for many months. We watched him grow in the Lord, as he secured a job, was able to finance himself, and even got married. He had a good baritone voice, and proved to be another stalwart in the church. We brought others in for shelter until they found their feet and got a job. We conducted prayer meetings daily from 4 to 6 p.m. We had a mixed congregation, as we did not only witness to blacks but also to whites.

Late one night, we had just come home from a meeting in North London, when I felt a strong compulsion from the Holy Spirit to walk around the block and shout "Repent, for the Kingdom of God is here. Repent! Repent! Fire! Repent!" Of course, it sounded like a madman gone berserk. "At twelve o'clock in the night, everyone will wake up. This is absolute madness. The police will be out!" However, I could not escape the constant pressure and urging of the Holy Spirit. I walked around the block, shouting as I went. As I came to a certain spot in Wiltshire Road and shouted "Repent!" a light came on and a window on the third floor flew open. "Oh-oh," I thought. "We've got problems here; I've upset somebody." Instead came a loud shout from a weeping woman, "Yes, Lord, I repent!"

Later that week, we made contact with the woman. She told us that since she had come from the West Indies she had been under constant harassment and disappointment. She could not endure any more. Just at that moment she was contemplating taking her life, when she heard this voice: "Repent! Fire! Repent!" She knew that God himself had come down to speak to her. She actually thought that it was the voice of God outside her window. One more life was saved through what seemed an act of madness: unorthodox evangelism, I totally agree. But the Holy Spirit knows when and how to reach the hearts of men and women. That woman also became a strong worker with us, playing the part of mother to the younger ones, always ready to give them a meal or a bed, to pray with them and to counsel them. We were now touching many people in the community; many who were lost in the big wide London world, bewildered, like sheep without a shepherd.

CHAPTER NINE

God gives me Muriel

Every afternoon at four o'clock, a group of us used to meet for two hours of prayer. We prayed for revival in Brixton, Kennington, Camberwell, Tulse Hill and Streatham. We surrounded the whole area with prayer, calling upon God for revival, week after week. Once a month we had a whole night of prayer. It was great to see up to thirty people packed into the room, praying all night and calling on God. We agonised for a supernatural breakthrough, an unprecedented move of God to change the hearts of men. We knew that behind all the injustices, the harassment, the deprivation, the struggles which people faced, there were demonic forces. It would take God's intervention in the affairs of men to change things. I have seen some answers to these prayers, but am still waiting and longing for a real trend-changing revival that will revolutionise our society.

At five one afternoon, six of us knelt in prayer quite deeply absorbed. Suddenly the door opened. Not knowing who had entered, I heard a voice saying to me, "Your wife-to-be has just entered the room!" I was too ashamed to open my eyes and look to see who it was. I felt I had transgressed the Holy God. Can you imagine my thoughts? Here we were, praying for revival, praying that God would break through and demons be defeated, and I was having thoughts of my wife coming into the room! I rebuked the Devil, I confessed my sin, I asked forgiveness, and I rebuked the Devil again. I was caught in an internal battle to free myself from my intense embarrassment and sense of uncleanness.

Then after a while I realised that I was fighting the Holy Spirit! It was not the Devil! I stopped and listened. I was half exhausted. As I listened to the Holy Spirit, I realised that God was seeking to communicate something to my heart. Reluctantly I relaxed, still not really wanting to believe because marriage and a wife did not figure in my plans. I just wanted to live for the sake of the Gospel. In any case, how could I afford to keep a wife? Furthermore, I was too young to think of these things. Maybe later when I had satisfied myself that I had done the will of God, maybe some time in the far future. Not now. But now I realised that this was not just the Devil, nor me. God was seeking to get my attention.

The meeting finished. Somewhat sheepishly I looked around to see who had come in while we were praying. Standing in a corner, head still bowed, was the same delightful, lovely looking lady I had seen at the baptism. There she was, Muriel Inez Leonara, my wife to be. Oh no! I felt so shy and silly, I did not even know how to approach her.

"Welcome to us," I ventured, hoping that my voice would not betray my conflicting emotions.

Three long months of struggle ensued. The fact that I was her pastor during this time made things more difficult. To remain objective and ministering, counselling her on the one hand and keeping my emotions at bay on the other was a giant test of my spirituality and integrity. She was of Jamaican descent, I was of Indian extraction: two different races, cultures and backgrounds – a compound problem. I had long thought that God had dealt with my prejudice. I really meant that, but as so often happens, we do not always know all that is deeply hidden within us until God puts us to the test. Although in theory I loved all men irrespective of colour or race, I was surprised and embarrassed by my reactions. I wanted to push them quickly aside. I was too embarrassed to admit that there were lingering racist attitudes and prejudices active within me, but now I just had to find out the truth about myself and face reality, so I allowed all the questions to surface.

"Lord, what will other people think? What about the children? Mixed children always go through a lot of hassle from others in society. In any case Lord, why can't I marry someone of my own race, if I have to marry? Would she understand me? How could I support her? Has she got a calling as well?" The arguments multiplied as the question arose. The more I sought to erect barriers and raise objections, the more the Holy Spirit would knock them down and convince me. I realised that God's choice was best. He had not been wrong yet. A straight question came to me from the throne of God as I prayed: "Shall I pander to your prejudices and give you what you desire, someone of your own race, or will you take what I give?"

Without hesitation, with tears of shame because I had been so stubborn and undiscerning, I replied: "Lord, I'll gladly take what you give; I dare not choose for myself."

I felt a tremendous sense of release, and a cleansing stream washed over me as I yielded and repented to the Lord. Glorious freedom.

After three months, I still wanted to be sure, not because of the race issue but because I still wanted to be sure I was not making a mistake. I said, "Lord, I am going to put out a fleece. I am seeking another confirmation, Father, just to be sure. Surely you understand this? Usually it is the man who asks, 'Will you marry me?' – I want to ask you the impossible. I'm going up to see Muriel today, and if it is really you, let her say to me 'I love you', first."

I took a long Green Line bus journey from Brixton to Coulsdon. I bought her a gift. For all she knew this was a pastoral visit. For me it was one big crisis. Not even knowing if she had an interest in me, I wended my way through the lane from the main Brighton-London Road, growing more and more apprehensive with each step. "Some major transaction will take place today," I thought. I had never had any girl friends or any relationship of this sort before, so I was just like a nervous schoolboy on his first date. She accepted my present, not quite knowing what to say. She introduced me to her friends and we chatted about church, about her work. She cooked a meal.

As the afternoon grew later we sat in the Common Room watching cricket on the television, West Indies versus England. Rohan Kanhai and Sobers were batting. Suddenly Muriel turned and spontaneously said, "Do you know that I love you?"

"How incredible!" I thought, as I struggled to maintain my composure and some modicum of equilibrium.

I said, "Lord, thank you." No more confirmation needed. My question answered, my prejudices dealt with; three months of struggle over.

"I love you as well. Will you marry me?" I blurted out with such conviction that it shocked her. She knew nothing of my struggle, but now I told her. She told me that she had also been struggling for three months. Apparently God was working at both ends of the candle at the same time. She accepted my proposal. We fell deeply in love. As we prayed with each other, God was very present. We knew that we belonged to each other, committed for life in a partnership to serve the Lord wherever he might lead us. Before we parted, I said to her:

"There are three things that you will have to pray about and consider. One is, to be prepared to live sometimes as a missionary widow, because of my frequent travels and involvement with others. Secondly, I will not be able to give you everything you need, and you will have to learn how to 'live by faith' and be willing to trust the Lord for all material things. Thirdly, it is important that you know that you have a calling to a missionary life as well."

As we kissed each other good-bye that night, I knew that God had spoken and had given me someone precious, someone to be treasured, who would be an asset and a friend. I wrote home to my parents to tell them of my engagement and proposed date of marriage, giving them a full description of my wife to be. I outlined the circumstances leading up to our engagement and how she was of African descent, born in Jamaica, five years older than me, training to be a nurse, same height as me, beautiful in my eyes. At the same time I wrote a letter to Muriel's mother who was her only surviving parent, asking for Muriel's hand in marriage. I received a very prompt reply from Muriel's mother, giving her full consent. I had told her that I was of Indian descent, born of Hindu parentage, a converted Hindu, that I had nothing much to offer her daughter, and that I was a full time missionary living by faith and trusting God for all our material needs. She seemed so happy, and wished us God's blessing. Two weeks after, we received a telegram that she had gone to be with the Lord. She was a believing Christian. We are so glad that we have at least that one letter. It is still in our possession, the only contact I had with Muriel's mum.

My own parents took a little longer to reply. A month or two afterwards a letter came. I had realised I was risking another series of tensions between them and me. They had accepted the fact that I had become a Christian, but now, to marry someone of another race and culture was equally unacceptable and unthinkable. They protested in their letter; they even threatened that if I went ahead and married Muriel, they would disown me this time. I suspected that it was a letter written in the heat of the moment. Nevertheless this hurt, for I loved them very much. I was relieved when a second letter came, written in a milder tone.

At two o'clock on 1st November 1958, I walked up the aisle at Stockwell Baptist Church to take Muriel as my bride. It was a pleasant dry afternoon, the sun barely peeping through an overcast heaven. There were seventy-five of our friends gathered round us. Friends to whom we had been ministering, friends whom I had met on the street and gathered into the bed-sit prayer meetings, stood in support and to wish us well. Prominent among them were my co-worker, Ken McCarthy and his family; Eva Carr, the nurse who led Muriel to the Lord and who became a very close friend and sister to us, and her husband Egerton; and Len Bellamy, my best man – a white English brother who has showed me much love and kindness. One day as I stood at Victoria Station looking lost, he had come and befriended me. He always made me feel welcome in his home, which often served as a place of rest for me. Dora, his wife, was a real big sister to us. She undertook all our prayer-letters for ten years. There were many other friends whom we cannot mention here.

At one thirty, while I was dressing for the wedding, I had realised that I had not got the one guinea to pay the Registrar. All along, we had been trusting God and he did marvellously supply. Muriel was still in nursing, so could have supplied her own needs. We managed together to find the money for the other expenses – the reception, the cake etc. But this one guinea never came. Maybe, I thought, I should have put that aside. I did not really feel that I could go now and ask any of my friends. I dressed and prayed. I pulled one sock on, prayed; pulled the other sock on, prayed; and waited, fully expecting that before I left the house for the church, the miracle would happen; but nobody came. What was I going to do? I started up the steps leading to the church. Halfway up the steps, Len came and pressed something into my hand. I pushed it into my pocket, without knowing how much it was. When I settled down, I had a quick look, and it was exactly one guinea. Again, God kept me waiting until the last minute, but he did not disappoint me. He provided.

It was my responsibility to find a place to sleep that night. As much as I tried, I could not find anywhere. So I kept waiting and praying, waiting and praying, right in the middle of the proceedings. The reception was a very happy and joyful occasion. Sometimes I took time off to breathe a quiet word of prayer: "Lord, I know you have somewhere for us to sleep tonight, somewhere to take my beautiful bride." It isn't that I liked living dangerously, or taking unnecessary risks without money; I really could not book anywhere. I didn't have an option. After the reception, while we were moving round and shaking hands with our friends, a dear white lady from Streatham, Mrs. Doris Field, a lovely Christian praying woman, said to me,

"Philip, you probably think this sounds crazy, but while I was praying today I felt God telling me to air out a room that I had closed up for years and to prepare it for you and Muriel to spend your first night together in my house. It is there if you need it." I was struck dumb, lost for words. God was thinking about us all along. He had gone before us to prepare a room. Once again just at the very last moment, he came to my rescue. He provided and did not allow me to be put to shame. What a loving Father! I had met Mrs. Field through our door-to-door work. She immediately adopted me and once every week we went to her house for prayer. She was a real mother.

After two weeks of honeymoon and holiday in Folkestone as guests of our friends Len and Dora Bellamy, we returned to one room in an unoccupied and dilapidated manse, loaned to us by the kind pastor of Stockwell Baptist Church. Later the others came and occupied the other rooms so that for a while the manse replaced Overton Road as our base. We had many lovely wedding presents from our friends in Sweden and England. We had no family, no relatives, just the friends we had made – contacts through our missionary work. Although they could not be substitutes for our loved ones whom we had missed very much on the day, they made us happy and did us proud.

We had pots and pans, cups and cutlery, but no furniture. There was an old bed-settee that was left in the room which we used as a bed. Well, the settee had seen better days and did not have a lot of life left – it was like sleeping in a hammock. It was real close fellowship those first months, whether we liked it or not! Later on we moved into Dulwich Road, which became our home and the centre for our work for five years. It was not our intention that Muriel should finish nursing just then; we really wanted her to finish midwifery and then decide whether the Lord wanted her to be full-time with me. We do not have a philosophy that to be involved in God's work you have to be working full-time, and not have a secular job as well. We appreciate fully that not all Christians live by faith, and not all Christians are full-timers as such. So, we were very surprised when the Matron called Muriel into her office and dismissed her from the hospital. Muriel was shocked, as she had been gaining good credits and was doing very well in her work. When asked the reason, the Matron simply said with some annoyance, "I do not have married nurses in my hospital."

'But you knew I was getting married," Muriel protested.

"Yes, but you should have known that married nurses do not work here." It was the first my wife knew about it! She came home dismissed and discouraged, her dreams of being a fully qualified nurse abruptly shattered.

CHAPTER TEN

Travels abroad

We were shocked at first, not so much because of the loss of income, but because it aborted Muriel's training. More than anything else that stunned us. As we sought the Lord about the matter, we decided not to worry about it any further, and received peace to pursue our partnership in the ministry together. Side by side we laboured therefore, my wife and I, Ken and his wife, and those whom the Lord had added unto us. The training programme was proceeding successfully.

An invitation came to send helpers and workers to Nigeria, Ghana and Liberia. Clarence, Bertrand and Johnson, three tall burly West Indians, two from Jamaica, one from Dominica, were chosen as the three musketeers to go to Nigeria. They were taken by Ken, initiated, and left to get on with it. The adventures of those three men would take another book to relate. They were caught up in the whole Biafran saga, and were there at the very height of the Civil War. The stories of suffering, mistaken identity, facing the firing squad, their narrow escapes – one brother actually buried his dear wife out there – would make interesting reading. We had seen these, our first missionaries, depart after a great valedictory service in St. Matthew's Church in the centre of Brixton. Four hundred people gathered to bid them farewell, to pray, and to send them: the first black missionaries sent from Britain.

In 1959, when our first daughter Pauline was just two

months old, an urgent request came for help from a dear
American sister, Maggie, who was a missionary in
Liberia. We met as a team, and decided that as Ken was
already heavily committed elsewhere, I should answer
that Macedonian call. I was accustomed to travelling
and being away from home, but this time it was
different. We were beginning to feel a real family, with
the closeness that Pauline brought to our lives, the joy of
being a mum and dad. The pain of leaving my young
wife and baby was a hard test, but we both had to
embrace the cross and offer up our own preference and
happiness, and count it as joy to serve others.

I arrived in Liberia, twenty-two years of age, as green
to the mission field as a young cadet. Maggie welcomed
me and schooled me in the ways of working in a different
culture. I had the joy of helping her in the young pioneer
work for three months. I preached in several of the
churches in Monrovia, with great blessing and results.
For one month I had the privilege of addressing the
senior high school which was administered by the
Methodist church. Every day at morning assembly,
straight Gospel preaching for one hour! Many of the
students accepted Christ during those days. I also had a
rare privilege, an invitation to minister one Sunday
morning in the Baptist church where the Vice President
and his family regularly worshipped. He was actually
one of the pastors of the Baptist church. That morning
service was unusual. I was fearful and nervous. There
were members of the cabinet, the Vice President and his
wife, and many other dignitaries. I wanted to turn and
run. There was no way I could escape, however. I stood
up and read from Romans chapter 13. I began to preach
falteringly and cautiously, then suddenly I felt the Holy
Spirit come upon me. Fear disappeared and words
began to come freely and fluently. Boldly I spoke, as I
felt urged and inspired. At the end of forty-five minutes,
the Vice President got up and said, openly weeping, to a

sobbing congregation, "Ladies and gentlemen, we have heard the word of God to us. I will be the first to respond. Join me in repentance." The whole church surged forward, including the dignitaries, and one hour afterwards they were still weeping and praying and repenting. God did many things that morning which only eternity will reveal. Afterwards, the Vice President and his wife invited me for lunch. As I sat at the dinner table and saw all the elaborate arrangements, I was very thankful that my friends in Barnet had taught me how to use a knife and fork; especially how to start at the outside and work your way in when presented with various courses.

The Vice President hugged me as he bade me good-bye, and said, "Any time you are welcome to come back to our country. I will see that meetings are arranged." I spent three months in Liberia with Maggie. Then another call came, from neighbouring Ghana. There was a group of American missionaries who had started a training programme. They asked me to come for a few months, to help generally in the work. I did not know that I needed a special visa and permission to remain in the country. It was in the days of Nkrumah the Great – he was at the height of his power. I remember seeing the obelisk in the centre of Accra, the capital, which said, 'Seek ye first the political kingdom, and all these things will be added unto you.' I felt anger and rage, the displeasure of God rise up within me, and I cursed that thing. I was not surprised when, a few years later, it was pulled down and desecrated.

One of the Americans could not accept that I, a black man from Guyana, had been invited by his colleagues to work with them for a while. Unfortunately he was the one who needed to write me a sponsorship letter for the immigration authorities. He refused, so, as I could not obtain a visa, the authorities called me in after a month and ordered me out of the country forthwith. I explained that I did not have money to purchase a ticket. Could I have a few days? "No, you must leave within twenty-four hours," came the reply. Impossible, I thought! But then again, all things are possible with God. I spent most of the next fifteen hours in prayer. Waking up early the next morning, I felt rather low and dejected, and thought, "Imprisonment is facing me." The immigration officer had explained that if I was not out of the country within twenty-four hours, I would be placed in prison, and subsequently deported. Emily, one of the missionaries, came to see me and asked:

"Why are you looking so glum today?" When I explained, she said, "Tell that serpent to get back on its belly, he has no right to get up and talk to you like that." She meant, of course, the Devil. She prayed with me, and that heavy, dark cloud of foreboding lifted. I went down to the immigration office prepared either for an extension or to be placed in prison. As I mounted the steps and entered the office, the officer enquired, "You still here?"

"Well, sir," I said, "I have not been able to purchase the ticket as yet, but I am waiting, and came to report my situation to you. I would be grateful if you could grant me a further extension."

"Impossible!" he said. Then he went to his superior officer. He came back and said, "We'll give you another thirty-six hours." We came down to the last six hours – still no money. Then a letter came through the post of that last day at about four o'clock in the afternoon, an unusual time for post to arrive. The letter stated that two weeks ago, whilst praying, the writer had felt constrained to deposit some money in my account, as he felt that I had a very special need at the time. Can you imagine my relief! I took the letter to my missionary friends, and asked if on the strength of this letter they could advance me the money for the fare. Once back in London, I would return it through a mail transfer to their bank account. They agreed. Having secured the money for the ticket, the problem now was to get to the ticket office before it closed. We arrived there half an hour after closing time to find that it was still open with a couple of people still lingering around, and we managed to get the only seat available on that night's plane to London. It had become available because of a last minute cancellation which reached the office moments before we walked in. So God delivered me from imprisonment and from embarrassment. He intervened just in the nick of time to prove once again his fatherhood and his care. Whether he was putting me through a serious test to see whether I would go on trusting him in this panic situation, I cannot tell. I know I did panic sometimes, and felt anxious and even worried. But through it all, I have learnt in crises that there can be calm in the storm, there is a place of safety and security in God even at really difficult times. "They that put their trust in the Lord, will never be put to shame."

As I reflected on the past four months during that night flight from Ghana, I asked myself again and again, was I ever to return to Africa? Would I ever have the chance of preaching the Good News of Jesus again in this vast continent? Was I leaving behind any lasting fruit? It is still my dream that, one day, I might meet some of those who accepted Christ. Who knows what stories we would have to tell when we meet one another in that long eternal day?

Indelibly printed on my mind was the vision of a little American black woman whom I met in Liberia who had gone out there, and was giving herself totally to three hundred children in a thatched roof, mud-floor building. She became a mother to those children, taught them school, looked after their social and health needs, and she was not even thirty years of age. She had a degree under her belt, but she loved the Lord and put his service first, and obviously loved every one of those three hundred children. Her life challenged me so much that I actually decided that I wanted to serve the Lord just as she was doing in the jungle village deep in the heart of Liberia.

In another interior village, I shared the Gospel with a young man who accepted Christ. His whole life changed, and he found joy unspeakable. His marriage improved, so he wanted to show me his gratitude. According to their custom, that meant treating me to one of their delicacies – in this case, a roasted bush-rat! It was to be a total surprise, but he was not too subtle about it and I found out. When I realised what was going to be my lunch that day, I prayed fervently. Oh, brother, I prayed! "Can I escape this rat?" I remembered Jesus's prayer, "If it be possible, let this cup pass from me." Well, I wasn't facing a cross, I wasn't asked to shed my blood, but everything inside me revolted, and refused to embrace that rat. Oh, I loved these people. I loved that man but I did not want a rat! I went into the nearby bush and prayed. While that rat was being prepared, I prayed. Once again the deep roots of prejudice that I did not know existed were surfacing. I did not know that such deep ugliness existed inside me. After many anxious, agonising moments, God got through to me, and I was able to say, "I love you enough, and I love that man and his people enough not to insult their hospitality. I will eat it." In fact, when later I went to 'dinner' under a tree, the fellow apologised for burning the rat carelessly and we ate something else. The Lord kindly accommodated my weakness, but nevertheless through a roasted rat I was drawn closer to these people, and to the King of Glory – the one who drank from the bitter cup, who became sin for us that we might become the righteousness of God. He knows what it feels like to be identified with mankind... My reverie was broken as I drifted away into sleep, winging westwards back towards London.

I arrived home in the early hours of the morning, not having had time to contact my wife beforehand. I arrived in a taxi. When she saw me there, dishevelled and unkempt, she thought she had seen a ghost. It was pure joy to be reunited. I distinctly remember my daughter Pauline, six months old, looking very enquiringly at Mum, when I started to settle in the room, as if to ask, "Who is that strange man, Mum? Where did he come from, who is he?" It didn't take too long, though, for us to get re-acquainted. Pauline, like my other daughters, has been a source of joy and inspiration to me. Anne appeared on the scene a year later, and Christine in 1962.

In November 1957, I was reminded of the invitation of the Swedish pastor some years before. I had long since dismissed the whole thing from my mind because when I had sought the Lord's will on this matter, I had received no positive answer. One day, suddenly and totally unexpectedly, whilst in prayer, I felt the Holy Spirit saying, "Write to those pastors, and tell them that you now feel confident to come, if they still so desire."

I was in Len's house. We had just had tea and were sitting by the fireplace, he on one side, I on the other. I had the letter in my hand preparing to go out and mail it. Suddenly, doubt gripped my heart and I said to Len: "This looks as though I am inviting myself, Len. I don't think that I will send this letter." I actually threw it onto the fire, whereupon Len, quick as a swordsman, grabbed it before it reached the flames, and said:

"If you won't post it, I will, because God is showing me that this is the right thing for you to do. I will post it." He hastily put on his coat, and went out.

Eight days later, a reply came. "Come immediately. We need you." So, I arrived in Sweden on 8th January. I will never forget that journey. I never realised how much colder Sweden was than England. I didn't have any suitable clothes or proper winter shoes, only an overgrown rain-mac, given me by a dear Baptist friend, Leslie Howard. The icy cold seemed to reach my very bones. But I was enthralled by the beauty of fresh-fallen, silver, glittering snow: miles and miles of it, hanging from the trees, just as you see it on Christmas cards. Rooftops covered, all nature clothed in beautiful white snow.

Eventually I reached my destination. Everything seemed so strange and new; a different climate, different atmosphere, and a different language. I was received at the other end by the burly pastor who had almost crushed me with his hug at Hyde Park. After a quick meal we rushed to the first meeting, in Vrigstad mission church. Next day he took me to one of the believers in the church who ran a gents' clothing shop. They took my old clothes and burnt them, and made a speech. They committed them to the fire, and said, "Rest in peace." They then proceeded to fit me out with shoes, coat, gloves and scarf. For the first time I had a new coat, suitable for the winter. It was good fun and I felt that someone cared.

We had many meetings, three campaigns, at the very height of the Swedish winter. It was part of their custom, during those winter months, to have indoor campaigns. I spent six weeks, two weeks in each of three different towns, and in each place the Lord blessed the ministry. People were saved and renewed, the sick were healed and in one place, many teenagers turned to God. According to the pastors years afterwards, "Revival came to our town." This began an association with these dear people, and opened up the door to much of Sweden. Little did I know then that God was preparing the way and opening the hearts of people who later on would become the main source of support to my wife and me. Surely God could have used others, but here we found mothers and fathers in the faith – friends who stood with us when we were well, when we were sick, when we were hungry, and when we had nothing; friends who wept with us, who prayed with us, who remained faithful to us through the years. Truly, God moves in a mysterious way, his wonders to perform.

I often think how strange it must seem, that a little black man from a sugar plantation in the deep south, should reach the very north of the world, to preach the Gospel to people who have known it for generations and who certainly could teach me a whole lot more. These were people with vast experience of the things of God. They have built churches, they have sent out missionaries. They have a Christian heritage and experience in church planting and evangelism, and yet I was feeling that God wanted me to get more involved in a meaningful way with these brethren – not just a one-off visit. I kept this in my heart for fear of appearing presumptuous. I said nothing about it to anyone. Then as we came to the end of that visit, I received a permanent invitation from the Swedish Alliance Mission leadership through Karl-Erik Andersson and Hilding Fagerberg, to travel with their tent which was assigned to the youth arm of that mission. So for three consecutive years, each summer, I spent four months travelling with this tent from city to city, as their evangelist – a time when I learnt much about work with young people. God did mighty things in these tent meetings. People accepted Christ. In a situation where miracles and baptism of the Holy Spirit were not popular, or even accepted in some quarters, the Lord moved in a supernatural way to demonstrate his love. I prayed for the sick, and other needs, and things happened which could not be denied. The leader of that mission himself came to see, to test as it were the soundness of what I was doing. He became a real friend and father until the day of his death a few years ago.

In 1963, by which time Muriel and I had come to

realise that God was calling us to go back to Guyana as missionaries, we spent six months as a family in a small cottage in a village called Rorvik, where by now we had many friends. They provided us with a home. Those six months were a vital time of preparation and ministry before we launched out to our new field in Guyana. I shall forever remain indebted to my many friends in Sweden who were instruments used by God to mould and to fashion my approach and some of my thinking and to temper my fanatical tendencies without blunting the radical edge and revolutionary concepts of my understanding of Christianity. These men and women adopted us as a family, and made us feel a part of what they were doing, without wanting to swallow us up organisationally. They provided us with a home away from home.

Early one summer morning in Rorvik, a brother came and knocked at the door. He was obviously distressed and in tears. When I enquired as to the nature of his business and the cause of his distress, he explained that he had not been able to sleep that night. He had tossed and turned, both he and his wife, uncomfortable all night. He was compelled to seek me out this early because God was speaking to him about supporting my wife and me. He felt urged and convinced that God was asking both him and his wife to donate one day's wages per week to us. This touched me very deeply because at that time I was asking God to speak to individuals, to stand by us with steady support. Curt and Britta were the very first ones, along with Leslie Howard in England, who faithfully supported us each month. We parted after a time of prayer, and he asked God to raise up many others who would share the burden not only for my personal support and income, but also for financing our future work in Guyana.

At about that time I was invited by a group of men, all in various positions of leadership, to lunch. One of them, a pastor and the leader of the youth mission, said that God would not allow them to rest until they did something tangible to support Muriel and me. There and then they initiated a group called the Guyana Friends. This group was not properly organised until after we first went to work in Guyana a few years later. Their support did not materialise for a while. Since then that group has grown, and has become one of the mainstays of our mission. Each year they meet to pray and to discuss fresh ways of increasing support. That group is still going, and fulfilling the task it was called to do, even though we personally are no longer in Guyana.

Sweden has meant a lot to me and to my wife and children. The lakes surrounded by majestic pine trees, the natural beauty of the countryside, the people, as well as the warm acceptance and love we have experienced, have filled many pages of our lives, and we shall always cherish them as precious memories. It was here that I was taught to drive a motor car. It was here that an older brother took me aside and taught me what little I know of theology. Here too I gained insights into pastoral work, and how to bring counsel to people in the real nitty gritty of their lives. They also generously opened up for me the inside workings of their mission, so that I could see how they were structured within the local churches, how the organisation and planning necessary to make the programmes work took place, and the value of proper planning. Solbritt and Albert Svensson adopted me as their black son and regarded me as a part of their family. Inga and Bengt Gunnarsson received us as their own flesh brothers and sisters. Hasse Broderna and Hakan are among my strong critics but faithful friends and encouragers. I have much for which to thank the Swedish Christians.

CHAPTER ELEVEN

The church grows in Brixton

Back in London, we needed more space for our work: space for counselling, space for the Sunday evening meetings which were growing steadily in numbers; space for the evening Bible study/night school which had grown to the point where we were considering starting a full-time training programme.

A significant development during this time was the spread of bed-sit prayer meetings around the city. Immigrants were scattering to Dalston, Stoke Newington, Tottenham, Battersea, Tooting and Balham, Streatham and Croydon. As they found jobs and purchased or rented flats and homes, they were moving out of Brixton into other areas. Here they experienced the same rejection and coldness in the churches as they had found by and large around Brixton. They encouraged many whom they contacted in the market places and at work to gather for prayer and they were greatly helped. Many of them still testify that the strength and support that they received from these simple meetings enabled them to survive. Had it not been for the encouragement received from these lay activities, many of these people would have been nervous wrecks and social liabilities – sad products of a system in which the newcomer was not welcomed. No provision seemed to be made to involve them in the life of the community or instruct them in the ways of a new culture or to integrate them into the main stream of the society. They were left to fend for themselves against formidable odds. Social workers were ill-prepared to handle and cope with the complexity of the needs of such an influx of people, as diverse as they were, and to integrate them into British middle-class culture and structures.

And so these bed-sitter gatherings provided a safe port and a haven. They were places of refuge, a weekly respite from the storm outside. By praying and interacting with people of similar backgrounds who were experiencing like hardships, these people gained the strength they needed to forgive those who ill-treated them. Through these meetings, they maintained contact with God, who filled their gloom with light and gave them hope for the days ahead. They learned the secret power of prayer, the art of taking everything to God. A whole network of bedsit prayer meetings sprang up wherever the immigrants settled. They were conducted mostly on Saturday nights. As a result of the people's energetic witness many of them expanded to thirty or forty people. This growth forced them out of the bed-sitting rooms and they had to find larger alternatives like unused church halls, community centres and shop-fronts. Some of them managed to group together to buy buildings which they converted into meeting places. These were no longer prayer groups, but developing congregations.

It is to the credit of the black community that they were not content to continue living in their little rooms, or to become a burden on the state for housing. Through their own industry and initiative they worked and saved, acquired mortgages and purchased houses, and moved into areas outside Brixton. They were not satisfied with remaining in a position of disadvantage. The sad thing is though that when black families moved into a street, they were not welcomed. They were harassed and bricks were thrown through their windows. If two or three of them moved on to a street, it was amazing to see how many 'For Sale' signs went up. The white population, instead of welcoming them and helping them to integrate into their society, moved out and away to avoid living near to the blacks. The more well-to-do elements of society moved out, some to other residential areas of London where there were very few, if any, blacks; others to the suburban and rural towns and villages. This left a vacuum which has not been filled to this day.

Among those affected were industries, businesses, and shop owners, who closed down and pulled out. The whole social, economic and religious life of these areas changed drastically. Vibrant communities were suddenly left deprived, without a heart, and empty. It meant that churches in the area gradually emptied and many of them closed down. Churches that had a hundred and fifty members suddenly found themselves down to twenty or thirty people and struggling to survive. In order to keep them going, people used to travel in to the Sunday morning meetings, and then travel back out to their safe suburban dwellings. The poor, the working class, the immigrants, were left in a community without the necessary substance to keep it cemented together. A sense of desolation slowly gripped many of these areas. Those who remained and the newcomers had to start all over again. It was pioneer work.

The congregations which had started as immigrants' prayer groups now grew, through vigorous evangelism and work with children and young people, into churches in their own right. Unfortunately, in spite of the best efforts of the West Indian churches to get white people to attend, it never happened. They were helped and blessed but they would not remain in the congregation or become part of the family. Actually, they were experiencing a kind of reverse reaction. There were not sufficient of their own kind, so they felt a minority within these congregations, even though no effort was spared to make them feel wanted and cared for. The black pastors would go out of their way to look after the white members of their flock, but they could not succeed in keeping them.

Of course, a West Indian liturgy, music and song played a very significant part in their worship. Their kind of music was loud, vibrant, full of rhythm. Rhythm is part of the make-up and personality of the blacks. It is in the blood. Music is a very special kind of language, and often the lively choruses communicated truth in their own peculiar way, far more effectively than preaching. It is the language of the heart, as it were. It is a means of communicating special truths from God to us. Singing is often accompanied by tambourines and clapping of hands, and punctuated by *Hallelujah!*'s and *Praise the Lord!*'s. There was a free, spontaneous expression of love to God and of gratitude for being set free from the bondage of sin; tears of joy, that the Lord was actually helping them to make something of their lives. So the meetings were filled with spontaneous joy, hilarious singing, shouts and exclamations. It was not unusual to find, in the atmosphere of joy and ecstacy, the whole church moving with the music, and dancing in the presence of the Lord.

This of course put off average, well-behaved, conservative, reverent English. The West Indian meetings consisted of large portions of Scripture being read, and hot fiery preaching of the Word, always followed by fervent appeals for people to repent, to rededicate their lives to God, to be healed, to answer the call of God for ministry. Of course, all these appeals would not happen in every single meeting, but it was usually an important part of the proceedings. The meetings also afforded an avenue for artistic expression, and so special songs, drama and competition, especially among the younger people, was often promoted. These activities provided healing to the black community, and helped to add some sense of worth and dignity to their being. That is the reason why so much of black music is centred in and around the church and the community.

In all this there was little or no attempt to hold the two strands of the black and white churches together. Each pursued its own direction and they kept to themselves. Very little attempt was made to explain the one to the other. No forums were held for discussion, no meeting or praying with each other. Each seemed happy to exist in splendid isolation. Being my brother's keeper did not seem important then. What a pity! At that time the traditional white churches suffered from declining numbers. They were dying because their members moved away and there was no dynamic evangelism to bring in newcomers. In the meantime, these new groups of black Christians were serious about praying and evangelising and were committed to their churches both in personal involvement and in giving financial support.

It was challenging to see how mothers would spend Saturday nights preparing their Sunday meals and their children's clothes, washing, cleaning and shopping in order not to miss the meeting on Sunday. The meeting place was filled with babies in prams; where mother went, baby went too. It was not unusual for babies to be changed and fed in the middle of the meetings. There were no special rooms for that. It was a family day out spent in the presence of God and in fellowship with the other brethren. The women especially should be commended for the tremendous sacrifices which they made, many times without the support of their husbands. Most if not all of them worked in secular jobs if they could find employment, yet found time to do all the chores in the home. They pulled heavy shopping baskets and babies in prams, working five and a half days a week to supplement their husbands' incomes, and yet managed to find the time for Sunday-school work, youth work, prayer meetings and Bible studies. I was often amazed that even when winter was at its bitter height they would persist in coming long distances in order not to miss the meetings. They did struggle. They struggled with the weather, with their overcrowded living conditions, they struggled with their health and with their duties, but they made it by prayer and determination, with more than a little help from God. Many of them stand as stalwart pillars, shining examples for the younger generation to follow. Many husbands deserted their wives and got involved with other women. They neglected their families and spent much time getting drunk in the pubs and clubs and in the betting shops. Some men undoubtedly despised their womenfolk as second rate creatures. There were houses which existed to provide black men with white women as a special delicacy – places run by un- principled and wicked men exploiting the misfortunes and loneliness of a people still fighting for survival.

As the congregations developed into churches, a new phenomenon was appearing on the black church scene. Many of the men and women who came from the West Indies in the early sixties had belonged to different denominations in their own islands. When, therefore, they began to discover one another in London, they formed their own denominational groupings – the New Testament Church of God, the New Testament Assembly, the United Pentecostal Church and many others. For many of us who started in the mid-fifties, this was a sad departure from the Spirit, and from the love with which we started. Our original intention was never to have denominational barriers, island barriers, or colour barriers erected. We felt that we were in the forefront of creating a new thing – a church that was alive, integrated, multi-racial, multi-cultural, diverse and yet united; a church that would not reflect its peculiar brand of doctrine or government, but would experience real *koinonia*, a sharing of life one with another. Unfortunately, loyalty to the different denominations, and the strong encouragement from the leaders back home, proved much stronger than appeals to an ideal in scripture. A multiplicity of churches were formed and promoted not only in London, but also in every other major city in Britain where black people had settled.

The government of each church was different, reflecting its constitution back home. The notion that there isn't any sense of organisation or government in the black church scene is really based on lack of knowledge. In fact there are probably stricter structures of government than would be found in most evangelical circles. For example, any young man or woman who showed promise or ability to preach, once they had proven themselves in the eyes of the leaders, would be designated an evangelist. Sitting in any West Indian Church you would be surprised by the various titles that are used. The people are actually taught to refer to one another according to their office and titles as a mark of respect. You may be forgiven for thinking sometimes that there are more officers in the church than there are members, but it is their system, and they have made it work over the past thirty years.

The black church in this country has grown so that it now has over four thousand pastors, three thousand congregations and a hundred thousand born-again, active members. It is sad, however, to note that what began as meeting a need for teaching and fellowship and for showing love, has developed into so many fragmented groups. One such group has a hundred churches and a full-time Bible School, and there are many other such, scattered around the country. In spite of all its imperfections and weaknesses, it is marvellous to behold and is definitely a great work of God.

Distinctive of the black churches are their annual conventions, each group gathering all its adherents, once a year, for a week of celebration. It is a time when the Gospel is preached, a time when the faithful renew their covenant with God and rededicate themselves to his service; a time of renewal and refreshing and of discovering the next step forward. These conventions are usually the high point of their year. There is one group that usually meets in Brighton, and their youth convention alone had four thousand people attending recently, and the number grows each year.

Another feature of the black-led churches is their musical concerts, which have been drawing large crowds in recent years, especially among the young, both black and white. The most well-known of these singing groups is the London Community Gospel Choir, but almost every black church has a choir and a music group that is worth hearing. They perform with credit, and see it as a special ministry, an art form, a language, a means by which to reach others with the Good News.

The pastors and leaders of the West Indian churches carry out a very vigorous pastoral and counselling programme. The value of these men within the black community should never be underestimated. They are fathers and patriarchs of the community, and act as a steadying influence. Their contribution to the socio-logical development of the people can never be repaid – truly they are worth their weight in gold. They deal with all sorts of marital and financial problems, they counsel in domestic upsets; they help the sick, the suffering and the aged, and advise in difficult dealings with the police or with career officers. What is even more outstanding and astounding is that these people are engaged in secular jobs, as their church is not able to pay them a full-time salary. How they do it, and still manage to put in so many hours to work for the church, is beyond comprehension.

Like the mustard seed in the parable, the black churches have grown into a significant force of evangelical Christians, with a spontaneity and vibrancy and dynamism which the white constituency of evangelical Christians need. Imagine what power for good we could be in the hand of God, if both communities could combine their resources and provide a prophetic witness to a nation that is in desperate need.

Out of a very insignificant beginning, out of the ashes of despair and the trauma of rejection, the black churches have emerged and they have grown. On the other hand, the white churches have found it increasingly difficult to fill and maintain their buildings, and tragically, the church authorities have sometimes thought it best to put them up for sale. It was a grief to many of us to see the buildings once built by the sacrifices of God's people and dedicated to the service of God, now sold to the highest bidder and used for all sorts of ungodly activities – sometimes even used as a base from which much 'anti-God' activity ensued. According to a recent survey, one church building each week is being converted into a mosque. It confused us. It became a matter of importance to these young emerging churches, to own and to operate from their own buildings. It was not just a matter of status but a matter of convenience. When this proved possible, it provided a focus point and gave them a certain sense of security and permanence. Now they could determine their times and meetings and activities without inconveniencing anyone or being inconvenienced. They wanted to get away from the poor second-class citizen syndrome. They acquired some of these redundant and often dilapidated church buildings at enormous prices, and set about rehabilitating them. Some of the renovation work done on these buildings is nothing short of a work of art. They refurbished and renovated them, transforming them from dark, grey, forbidding-looking buildings and adding some colour and light to the decor to reflect their own kind of life in God and their worship. They had to take out enormous mortgages, and for this they raised thousands of pounds from their congregations in direct sacrificial giving.

Some of the stories are very touching and challenging. Some members gave their entire savings, some women worked long and hard to sew, knit, bake or do craftwork and then sell their produce, the proceeds going to the building fund. One of the reasons why their pastors are not paid is simply that they are still paying off their debts and loans. It is not because they are not a giving people – indeed their record books show that they are a generous people. Many of the churches are now using these buildings, so sacrificially acquired, as bases for propagating the Gospel; they also carry out programmes of Social Concern to reach and help the community. They have day schools, care for the aged, training programmes for young people, and even schemes to provide jobs for the unemployed in their churches. An outstanding example of this is a group of young men who converted a bus garage into a multi-purpose scheme for the young in Brent, north-west London. The properties are not just being used for church meetings, but are being used as centres for outreach and social action within the community. They have been restored to serve as beacons of light and centres for reaching the lost and dying. Acquiring these properties was a real venture of faith.

In my own case, when we were faced with a growing work, we had no funds with which to purchase a property. Nevertheless, I was so convinced that God who had called us was able to provide, that I went out in faith looking for somewhere suitable. I was walking along Dulwich Road, one of my usual visitation/street evangelism areas, when I noticed a 'For Sale' sign planted by the gate of a stately looking building. It looked as though it had just been refurbished. Judging from the outside, it seemed large enough to accommodate our needs at the time. As I stood and gazed at the building, I felt an inner witness from the Holy Spirit that God wanted it for his use. This was God's choice. I said to myself that there was no way that we could purchase a building that size, don't get excited, take it easy! Anyway, even though I could be wrong, I knew that Ken and his wife were far more experienced than I in matters like these, so I rushed to find Ken and shared with him what I had just seen.

CHAPTER TWELVE

The church established, we move on

Ken was also looking and searching, hoping that we might find something suitable. He was as excited as I was. He came and looked and said, "If only we could get it. It seems just the sort of thing we need." I quickly agreed. As we stood there looking at each other, each knew what the other was thinking: we were crazy to think we could get hold of a building like that without money. Then with a twinkle in his eye and a smile on his face, Ken said in a very determined voice: "God is able to give it to us."

Next we did what must have seemed very unusual to say the least – a very crazy thing. We marched up to the entrance together, laid our hands upon the green front door, and claimed the building in faith. As we prayed, there was a strong witness of God in our hearts, and tears in our eyes. After we had prayed and were walking back down the steps, a vision broke in upon our consciousness: a vision of a centre of evangelism, missionary activity and training; a centre for reaching the regions round about, and even for reaching other parts of the world; a place that would be filled with songs of praise. As we walked back from number 23 Dulwich Road, the reality of what we had just done dawned upon us. We checked up that evening, to find that we only had forty pounds between us. Forty pounds to buy a building many times beyond our capability. However, we had made an open commitment of faith, and we were convinced that there

was only one way for us: forward. We had no other
option.

We contacted the estate agents. The place was still
available. We made an offer which was accepted. A few
days later we placed a 10% deposit to start negotiations.
We were very excited. We prayed and shared with the
people and our friends. Our people offered, and others
also gave. Joan gave all her savings. Muriel had some
gratuities which she also gave. Eva and many of our
friends joyfully stood with us. By the time the solicitors
were ready to sign the contract, we had all but £125 of
the £5,000 needed to complete the transaction. The time
drew near. No more money. The night before, Muriel
and I prayed. My friend and co-worker, Ken, had
departed for Sweden where he was due to take a
crusade, a couple of days before. As we prayed that
night, I realised that in a few hours I would have to find
this money. Next morning I woke up and rushed to the
door, thinking that the postman must have brought
God's answer. Nothing: my face fell. I rushed to a book
shop where some of our mail used to come: nothing there
either. I lingered in the shop. There was a promise box
sitting on the display table. I was not really accustomed
to draw promises, but I just felt I had to pick one of these
and like a timely greeting from God, read the words:
'Jehovah Jireh – the Lord will provide.'

The hours were ticking away. I would have to reach
the solicitor by two o'clock, or else the whole transaction
would be off and we would lose our 10%. Agonisingly I
prayed and waited: "Lord, I don't really know how you
will provide, but I believe your word; I know you will
not fail me." Suddenly I felt an urge to go and ask the
state of our balance at the bank, even though I had been
there only yesterday and had been told that we had
exhausted all our funds. It persisted: "Go to the bank.
Go to the bank."

Eventually I obeyed. I was thankful that it was one of

those high counters, so that my trembling knees were hidden! With some trepidation, I asked the clerk, "Can I see the state of our account, please?"

"Why? There's nothing more than what you saw yesterday. Haven't you completed that business yet?" he continued.

"No, Sir", I said rather faintly.

"Why?" he enquired.

"Well, we are still short of £125," I replied with some embarrassment.

"Hold on a sec. I'll just check," he said as he disappeared. He came back with a smile on his face.

"But you have money here!" he informed me.

"Have we? How come? Yesterday we didn't have it!" I said, choking back my excitement.

"Ah," he said, "I'll check again."

"Please make sure," I said. I didn't want to write a cheque for money we didn't have, and run into problems with the Bank Manager. He went in and checked with his supervisor, then came back and assured me, "Mr. Mohabir, the money is here all right. Someone came in this morning, and deposited this amount before you got here."

A spontaneous hallelujah was in place. While I was in the bookshop, waiting and praying, God sent someone to deposit just the amount we needed. It was with great relief that I signed the contract and handed over the cheque and received the keys. I hastened to send a telegram to Ken with just one word on it – 'Victory'.

A few days after, we took possession of number 23, Dulwich Road. It was a great day for us all. It was used as a centre for the work until 1976, and much of our vision for it came to birth and fulfilment. Ken and his wife occupied the top flat, and Muriel and I occupied one of the rooms on the second floor for a while, moving later as our family grew to two rooms in Norwood which we rented from the lady who had cried out that night

when I shouted in the Brixton street, "Repent! Repent!"
The other rooms and ground floor were designated for
the others who were with us in the residential training
programme. The basement was converted into a chapel
which could seat a hundred people. It did not take very
long before that chapel was packed to capacity.

Meanwhile in Somerleyton Road, on the same site
where Ken had successfully conducted a crusade several
years before, we erected a pre-fab building which had
been given to us by a free evangelical church that closed
down. We pulled it down, and re-erected it on that same
bombed-out site. We continued our work there also, and
it too was filled, especially in the evening meetings. The
training programme took off very slowly at first, but
increased from three to twenty students within a year.

Before I describe more about our work in Brixton, let
me recount one episode to do with accommodation that
mystified me, and still does. In 1960 even number 23
became too crowded – by now we had trainees from
many different parts of the world. Jim Parnell and Alan
Fleming, two English friends who took a keen interest in
the work we were doing, heard of a large house in the
countryside near Worcester which was ideal to develop
as a conference centre and large enough to house our
training department, with camping and other facilities
for young people. I still remember the big oak tree
outside the front of the house, and the green fields
stretching as far as the eye could see. After prayer we
really thought it was right to go ahead and purchase it
for the development of our work. Jim and Alan and
another family put a lot of money into the project, and
we were given possession, promising to pay the balance
in four months. Eventually we heard that a certain
business man felt led to give us the money that was still
needed. This was great news. What a wonderful
provision! But there was one condition attached to the
offer. "What could that be?" we wondered.

The condition was very simple: I and the students with me must move out within a few weeks of the completion of the deal. This was a shock. But why? No-one was prepared to tell me. Did I do something wrong? After discussing the matter without making any progress, I realised that I was becoming defensive. Clearly there was no room for negotiation. He had the money; I did not. Our time had expired. We must pay now or lose all. My world seemed to be crumbling under my feet and the whole vision for an international outreach and training centre collapsed around my ears. I was only twenty-four. What would I do with twenty students, three couples, my wife and children? I felt weak and hollow as I listened. If only Christian people and the Lord's work were less complicated! But there was nothing for it; I had to go.

Three weeks later, Alan and I borrowed a Bedford work bus, loaded up and took all our gear and ourselves back to 23, which was now more crowded than ever. This episode has remained a mystery to me ever since. Was there a sin on my part, a wrong, an offence? Did I not hear God on this matter? I was so sure I did! Was it my vision, or my doctrine which was at fault? They assured me it was not. Why would they not tell me? Was it because I was black? I must confess that the idea of my colour did enter my head, especially when my wife was told that she was crazy to remain married to me. We were saddened and hurt by the whole affair. Muriel and I have always been friends and we do love each other. We knew that someone somewhere was reading us very wrong. My heart was broken and I felt crushed, but Muriel and Eva and Ken helped me, and we soon picked up our work in London again as though we had never been away, with the training, the door-to-door visiting and the preaching in the Brixton market.

I must tell you about the most exciting experience we had in the market. One day as we started to sing, a white man came rushing out of a nearby store, warning us not to preach about Jesus. He did not want to hear. Then he disappeared. We ignored him and continued to sing and to preach. Our team was a real cultural mixture. People stopped and took notice. As one of the sisters was testifying, the same man came rushing up with a pistol in his hand this time, his face angry and violent. He came right up to us and stuck the tip of his pistol up my nose and said, "Mention Jesus one more time, and I'll shoot your brains out!" I didn't know what to do. I was staring death in the face not only for myself, but also for the young trainees who were standing with me. I was responsible for them. I implored them to call on the name of Jesus. As they did so, the man repeated:

"One more mention of Jesus and I'll shoot!" Should I be diplomatic, compromise, apologise? No. Suddenly, fear had gone. I looked him straight in the eyes and said:

"Jesus loves you!" Three times I repeated it. Each time I said it, I knew that the finger that was poised on the trigger could blow my brains out. When I said it the third time, "Jesus loves you", the man fell to the pavement, gun in hand, crawled his way out beneath the feet of the gathering crowd and vanished. By this time, hundreds had gathered round to witness the drama of Jesus demonstrated before their very eyes. They stayed on and listened while we found new courage to testify and sing our praise to God. Never before had such a big crowd gathered at any of our open air meetings on that spot.

Week after week we came back, and people would now come on purpose to hear us – people from the various islands of the West Indies as well as from many other countries. Brixton market is very international and sells foodstuffs which people are used to back home, so people from many races come there on a Saturday to shop. We acted as a contact point for them, and had great joy in accepting many who came to know Jesus through our meetings into the fellowship of the Church.

We also convened an Easter conference each year in Gresham Road Baptist church, which used to be filled to capacity with a wonderfully international and inter-denominational congregation. Many people came into the baptism of the Holy Spirit. Many were exposed to teaching on the New Testament Church. It was so new and different in those days. Many were ministered to by the gifts of the Holy Spirit, which were hardly accepted then and were even considered heresy in some quarters. People were not only blessed and refreshed, but they were hearing new things, revelations that were very much in embryonic form. We gave teaching on church government, gifts of the Spirit, the ministry of prophesy, spontaneity of worship, the unity of the body of Christ, and the need for the body to be built on good relationships. These were all truths that we were seeking not only to teach, but to implement amongst ourselves.

In 1962, Michael Harper preached for us, after he himself had received the Baptism of the Spirit in another setting. Jim Parnell and others shared the ministry. Black and white. It was lovely. Bryn Jones walked into our meeting, and was introduced to us by Jim Parnell. Bryn was single at that time, just out of Wales Bible College, and successfully conducting Renewal meetings in Cornwall and Devon. We became friends, and felt that God was joining and knitting our hearts together to form a team.

After that Easter convention in 1962, I felt that God was directing me to return to Guyana. Six years before in my little basement sanctuary God had given me a vision of several places in Guyana and the West Indies, and now I was feeling that he wanted me to do something about it. I shared this with Bryn some time later. His face lit up as he said:

"That's strange. I too have a feeling that God wants me to go into that area for a while. Any chance of our going together?" I was delighted, and we parted feeling sure that God was leading us. Muriel and I shared this direction with Ken and Joan and the other leaders. They all said Amen, they were sure that it was right.

We began making preparations to leave. It had been a great blessing working with Ken and the others in the team and it was a wrench to leave them. But we submitted to the will of the Lord. So Bryn and his new wife Edna, my wife and three children and I departed for Guyana. For me it was a return to my roots and beginnings, to take up the challenge of pioneer work, church planting and evangelism; for the others, including my wife who was from Jamaica, a totally new experience.

CHAPTER THIRTEEN

Guyana, here I come!

I packed a few belongings, some books and a public address system in a couple of boxes as best I could with the assistance of our dear friend Egerton Carr. Eva and Egerton have stood by us all along, encouraging and supporting us to obey God whatever the cost. Eva, you remember, was the nurse who led Muriel to the Lord. Their home was always open to us, and it was no coincidence that it was from their home that we departed for the mission field. They were like a real brother and sister to us, different though our backgrounds were.

I wrote to Harry Das – the Christian man whom I had met on the train in Guyana years before, my very first Christian friend – telling him that I was returning in April and bringing my family and the Joneses with me. He was still involved in full-time ministry in Guyana, especially among the Hindus and Muslims. He was pioneering in the villages in the Corentyne district, on the far eastern borders with neighbouring Surinam. I explained that we were not being sent out by any missionary organisation but were coming in answer to a call from the Lord, expecting to be involved in pioneer evangelism and church planting. I also mentioned that our main burden was to preach the Gospel in areas where there was no witness. I suggested that if it were possible we would like to serve the work of any churches or ministries already functioning in the nation, rather than importing any western-style denomination. We were thinking of an initial period of three years.

I also wrote informing my parents that I was returning with my family and another couple. We decided together that since we could not afford for all of us to fly, Bryn and Edna, Muriel and our three little girls should travel by boat, which would take three weeks, and I would fly. By going ahead, I could seek accommodation and make some preparations to receive them. There was also a lingering fear that troubled me and caused me some anxiety. I was not sure what reception I would have, coming home to my family with Muriel and the girls. Would it be cold, hostile or friendly? I could not tell. One part of me knew that my parents and family would conduct themselves with honour, while on the other hand, I knew I had insulted their pride and twice heaped on their heads what was considered a thing of shame, first by adopting another religion, and then by marrying into another race. I hoped for the best but feared the worst. I decided to steer a cautious course. Discretion was the better part of valour, I reasoned. In the event of there being any embarrassment or unpleasantness, it would be better to risk my own neck: face it alone and accept full responsibility for my actions rather than expose Muriel and the girls. They set off first, and on 3rd April 1964 I waved the six of them goodbye at Southampton, watching the boat pull slowly away from the harbour and then disappear into the late afternoon mist, leaving a trail of bubbles as the large propellers churned the murky waters up, ploughing a straight path to Georgetown, on the other side of the world. I stood there and watched them vanish. Tears filled my eyes and I wished I was there on board with them.

Next day I boarded my plane at Heathrow, bound for Georgetown. Eight years of adventure away from Guyana were now behind me. It felt like a chapter being closed. Years filled with experiences and memories I would not wish to change, and yet I could not help wondering if anything had been accomplished that would stand the acid test of time. Was there anything of eternal value? The endless rows of doors on which I had knocked, the street meetings, the pub escapades, the tent meetings in different places, the open-air meetings in Brixton market, the hard work in Somerleyton Road amongst the drug addicts, prostitutes and alcoholics, the teaching sessions and churches founded. Would anything of real consequence remain when all men's work will be tried by fire? Ah well, I thought, it's too late now. Those with whom we have laboured and invested most of this last eight years must continue the work and I must concentrate on my new assignment. Guyana, for better or for worse, here I come!

It is an almost unbelievable contrast. The journey from Guyana to London then had taken me nearly twenty-one days. Now in less than a day you can change climate, physical environment, the lot. My mind worked overtime. My imagination ran riot: "Will anyone be at the airport to meet me? What are they planning?" I longed for a peaceful and happy reunion. "How will I re-enter my village? Will Mum and Dad be there?" Ah, how I longed to see them! "Will I recognise my younger brothers and sisters? They must be so grown up by now! Will they know me?"

These thoughts played in my head, sometimes creating excitement, at other times generating anxiety. Deliberately I interrupted this train of thought to concentrate on wider and more important matters in relation to our mission to Guyana and the West Indies. The four 'prop' engines hummed with a monotonous droning sound as we sped across the Atlantic. With every passing hour I was being transported closer and closer to a new beginning, to start another chapter of my life.

"Where would we live? Are houses easy to obtain? We have no guaranteed support – no regular income that we can rely on... What strategy would we employ to accomplish our goals?" More questions there than answers. As I reflected on these things, I remembered two separate incidents: the vision God had given me in my basement sanctuary in December 1956, and an occasion in early 1963 on the banks of a canal in France, sitting in a car with Bryn Jones...

When I received the vision in 1956, I had been deep in intercession, pleading for God to move in different parts of the world. The section of the globe for which I was praying that night was the Caribbean and South America. After about three hours, exhausted and sensing that I had been wrestling with strong demonic powers over this region, I just relaxed, still kneeling by my bedside, a blanket lightly wrapped around me. Suddenly I felt Jesus entering the room. The atmosphere changed and became charged as it were with a Holy energy and yet a sweet sense of gentleness pervaded every corner of my small room. An awesomeness overwhelmed and filled me and I knew the Lord had come to communicate something important. I saw the archipelago of the West Indies neatly stretched out between the two Americas with its many islands arising out of the deep blue Caribbean waters like sparkling jewels in a dark night. At intervals, certain of these islands glowed as with a light flashing on and off. I reached for a map of the Caribbean which was included in the very first copy of a Christian monthly published in Kingston, Jamaica, called the *Caribbean Challenge*. I sought to locate these flashing lights and drew circles round them: Jamaica, Dominica, Barbados, Trinidad, Curaçao. What could this mean? I waited expectantly.

"These places are in my plan for your life," I understood him to communicate. Then the map of Guyana unfolded before me and, as in the former picture, the same flashing light illuminated eleven areas in Guyana: Skeldon/Springlands in upper Corentyne, Rosehall in lower Corentyne, New Amsterdam on the east bank of the Berbice River, Buxton on the east coast, Georgetown on the east bank of the Demerara river and Leonora/Anna Catherina on the west bank, Vergenoegen/Parika on the east bank of the mighty Essequibo river, Bartica, an island town sixty miles up the Essequibo, known as the gateway to the interior, Mabaruma on the north-western border with Venezuela, Moruka – a district with hundreds of miles of rivers running through thousands of square miles of dense tropical jungle and swamps; also unidentified villages on the east bank of the Demerara river on the thirty-mile stretch between the airport and the city of Georgetown. Again I paused: "What meaneth this?" These I understood were to be the strategic areas to be reached in Guyana.

The incident in 1963 was an equally unforgettable experience. Bryn and I had taken an afternoon off to pray and wait upon God for some instructions regarding Guyana. We were conducting two weeks of special meetings in an evangelical church in France. It was the first time Bryn and I had actually teamed up together. The Lord worked some outstanding miracles. Bryn had received a word of knowledge about a woman present at the meeting who was in deep sorrow because a loved one was seriously ill in hospital. She came up with tears, and we prayed, "Lord, distance is no barrier to you. In Jesus' name heal . . ." The next night there was great rejoicing as the person walked into the meeting. Now we sat by the bank of this canal and prayed. I shared with Bryn the vision God had given me years before, wondering if it had any relevance for the work we now felt called to in Guyana. We both felt confident that this was the plan to follow, but it was too big for us. How would we possibly be able to do all this? Then had come some very important instructions from the Book of Joshua, chapter eight, verses 3-5:

1 Choose men
2 Instruct and train them
3 Send them
4 Take them with you...

We were now into the second half of the flight. As I continued to meditate on what might be involved in making that early vision a reality, I found myself admitting three possibilities. Either I was a madman, or a hopeless dreamer, or else God was leading us into new dimensions of faith, and opening doors which would bring us into an interesting and exciting few years. The prospect both challenged and frightened me. As at other times when faced with difficult situations from which there seemed to be no easy way out, I resorted to prayer. I pushed the button on the arm of my seat and reclined, still meditating, praying, and wondering what progress the others were making. Overcome at last by the hectic activity of the past few days, I must have drifted off into the Land of Nod.

I woke up as the last meal was being served before landing. It was now dusk. After the meal I sought in vain to compose myself. In another few minutes we would land. I was nervous and filled with apprehension. Mixed emotions tore at my heart: a sense of joyous expectation at the very thought of seeing them all again, then a fear of being rejected, a forgotten son abandoned in disgrace because of the choices I had made to follow Christ, to be obedient to his call, and to marry Muriel. I was not ashamed of any of these decisions, only fearful of what they might now mean, but I drew strength and courage from the knowledge that the choices I had made were right in line with God's will and purpose for my life.

"Fasten your seatbelts in preparation for landing..." came the long-awaited announcement. A few minutes later we touched down. I steadied my nerves and braced myself, and followed the line of passengers as we filed out into the pitch darkness. It was like stepping into an oven at first. I had almost forgotten how hot and humid it can become. As we made our way to the immigration hall I noticed the shadow of a man leaping over the barrier as we were approaching. In the darkness I could not recognise who he was and wondered what he was doing. He carried himself with a degree of serious intent. As he came nearer, I thought, "It cannot be... Is it? No, it cannot be my brother!" He rushed towards me with open arms, we embraced each other, tears freely flowing. It was my brother George, unable to wait. Eight years was long enough. Police came quickly after him to escort him back to the barriers, but not before he had time to whisper: "Do not be afraid, all is well. We are all here to meet you."

I do not think he really knows to this day what an effect those words had. A great sense of relief swept over me and rivers of tears flowed freely, hidden only by the dark night. Tears of joy. We reached the little shed which served as the terminal at that time and went through immigration into the customs hall to await my luggage. I peered through the wire netting into the waiting crowd hoping to spot my mom and dad. The crowd seemed excited, waving their hands as if to attract the attention of someone inside. I looked behind me to see who among my fellow travellers they were beckoning to. Then, as I turned back, in a blundering flash of revelation I spotted my mother still frail as I remembered her, neatly dressed, joy written all over her beautiful face, and my father standing beside her with a quiet dignity as he always did, but unable to disguise the excitement in his brown face and the smile showing through his neatly trimmed moustache. Then it was like the unfolding of an album, one brother after another, and mingled with them, friends I recognised from the village. "Surely they did not all come to welcome me?" I reasoned within myself. But they had.

As I stepped out into the open crowd I was surrounded, embraced, hugged and kissed again and again: Dad was weeping, Mom would not let go of my arm. Half walking, half lifted into thin air, I was bundled into a car with my mom and dad and sisters. With shouts of welcome still ringing in my ears we started the hour-long drive to our village. I looked back through the rear window and realised that no less than eight cars were following us in convoy. We reached the village at about ten that night. I was in a dream world as I recalled so many things of my boyhood. I had seen so much in the wide western world, but somehow this little village with its unpaved roads, its trenches with stagnant water, its cows and sheep and mosquitoes, its houses built on stilts, this village with no electric lights, was home. Yes, this was home. The car turned into our street. The excitement mounted but I was totally unprepared for what was to follow. Facing the car was a whole mass of people. The path was blocked. The car doors flung open and I was lifted onto the shoulders of two men. I did not quite know what was happening. It was pitch dark. Was this the end? I looked around and tried to take in the scene. There were heads everywhere, and shouts of welcome, "Thank God you've come back!" I quickly concluded that this was a friendly crowd. The whole village was there, it seemed. Then I realised that the two men bearing me were my uncles. What a miracle!

After a few minutes we reached our front gate. It looked different. They had made a lot of improvements. There were even flowers in the front garden. There were people everywhere, inside and out. Completely over-whelmed I thought, "This is too good an opportunity to miss." Being let down and somewhat calmer now, I found a good vantage point on the steps leading to the front door. I thanked them all for the warm welcome so undeserved, and assayed to witness to the goodness of the Lord.

"Tell us more!" they shouted, as I retreated inside. The crowd eventually dispersed after a few hours. My third brother Cecil Seeram pulled me aside to one of the bedrooms and fell on his knees and pleaded, "Lead me to Jesus. I cannot wait any longer. I have been longing for you to come home to do this." My own brother – the first convert within the very first few hours. Praise the Lord! he was obviously ripened fruit. None of us in the family slept that night. They wanted me to relate everything that had transpired in the eight years I had been away. They wanted every detail. I did not think it wise to reveal everything for fear of distressing them too much. The negative things were not important, after all.

During my absence much had happened in my village. God had raised up Harry, one of my uncles who had been very sick but was miraculously healed. This caused another stirring and breakthrough for the Gospel, which obviously had its roots in the early days of my conversion. They had already planned one week of campaign meetings for me to preach. The crowds came night after night and many responded to Christ, among them several members of my own immediate family.

Two weeks later, Muriel and the others came and there was a repeat performance on a smaller scale. I stood waiting for them to come through at the harbour, confident now of my folks' attitude and their acceptance of Muriel. Her fears were swept away as both Mom and Dad welcomed her with a warm embrace. "I receive you as my daughter..." Mom continued, and they both fell on each others shoulders and wept. All uncertainty was behind us now. The stage was set for a new relationship. If any doubts remained Pauline, Anne and Chris made sure that they were swept aside. They won everybody's hearts. They took to their grandparents as if they had known them all their lives. No-one could be a happier grandma than my mom that night.

Bryn and Edna looked on patiently and waited. I think they were more than a little surprised when they were welcomed not only to Guyana but also into a family. For a whole week afterwards friends and neighbours from the village took turns to come home to pay their respects and welcome Muriel and the children, and from that time onwards Muriel became part of the family and the village. I was over the moon on two counts; my fears of rejection from my family were unfounded, and I was reunited with my dear wife and children. Together with Bryn and Edna, we could now begin our mission.

CHAPTER FOURTEEN

Guyana story

Harry Das had already negotiated to rent an old colonial-type house, situated at the corner of Waterloo and Murray streets, right in the middle of Georgetown. It was an old house, with three floors. It needed a lot of repair, and was infested with woodworm, cockroaches, and rats. But, it was just within the reach of our finances and our faith. Rental was very high, even though we shared it. We could not afford to rent the whole house, so we sublet the top floor to a young couple and we occupied the second floor. Bryn and Edna had one room, my family and I the larger room, and Harry occupied a makeshift room, which we hastily constructed in part of the sitting room. On the ground floor, part was converted into office space, and the other part into a meeting room. Two weeks before Bryn and Edna arrived, I knocked up some cupboards in the kitchen and made a bold attempt to create some comfort and make it more convenient for Muriel and Edna to cope. We used most of the money that we had between us to purchase a Volkswagen bus and some basic furniture – beds, tables and chairs. We had been there less than a month when we woke up one morning to find that someone had put us to sleep by spraying us with chloroform, and had emptied our sitting room of all the furniture that we had bought only a few days before. They also swiped my only suit, and my much-loved red Parker pen which had been given to me when I first left

Guyana. I have never seen it again.

I admired our two women for the way they adjusted to their new situation. Edna had never been to a foreign country before, and Muriel had left home when she was only a teenager. After eleven years in Britain, having to adjust to life in Georgetown with three young children was not exactly easy. Very often, there was very little in the cupboard, but they bravely managed to keep us and the children going, and to keep smiling. Women of prayer and of faith, they were a tremendous help and encouragement to one another, and to us. Edna and Muriel were like sisters, real good friends. They had to be, living as we did, almost on top of one another. Christine became Bryn and Edna's favourite. At times, I thought I had lost my little daughter to my two good friends. The children also enjoyed their new-found grandparents and uncles and aunties. My home village was fifteen miles out of the city, so we found opportunity to be with them, and they came often to visit us. We received very little financial support from England, or from anywhere else for that matter, but our faith kept us going. God supplied our needs, even though there were anxious moments.

We arrived in Guyana in 1964 at the height of the civil war between the Indian and African races who lived there. The nation was in the throes of the political struggle for freedom and independence. Guyana's population is divided into six races. The three main groups are those of African descent, those of Indian descent, and the original people of Guyana – the Amerindians. There are also smaller groupings of Chinese, a few whites, and those of mixed race. The two main groups, 43% Indians, 39% Africans, were divided politically along racial lines. The two parties were headed by an Indian – Cheddi Jagan, and Linden Forbes Samson Burnham, an African. These two men had started out in the late nineteen forties and early fifties as partners. They were largely responsible for the political awakening in our nation. They had co-operated in creating in the people a sense of nationalism and a desire for independence from Britain. Together with the trades union leaders, they did much to educate the populace and to raise the standard of living. Through Parliament and through industrial action they introduced laws and programmes that improved the working conditions of a lot of our people. In 1948 they had staged a nationwide strike in the sugar estates. I remember it well. I was just eleven years old. I still remember how the police raided the village and beat up the people. One fateful day, five people were shot down. The strikers were marching on a factory situated between two villages, where sugar cane was converted into sugar. Whether or not the police panicked and thought that the men were going to wreck the factory, we do not really know, but five people were shot dead. We had never seen such ghastly and desperate action. Five men, including one of my cousins, were killed: the first martyrs in the industrial struggle in our living memory. We had heard of other martyrs during the days of slavery, who rose up against their masters and almost wrenched victory from their colonial over-lords, only to be defeated by internal rumblings amongst themselves.

But then in 1953 something tragic happened. The two men went their separate ways and built their own parties. Unfortunately, they exploited the race issue in order to secure support. At the time we arrived, between 1963 and 1965, the tension escalated beyond a war of words. Violence erupted. There were bombings and burning down of homes. If there was a racial minority in a village, the majority would come together to burn their homes and chase them out of the village. There was action and reaction, reprisals and recriminations. It was widespread throughout the coastlands. Although by

now Guyana had internal self-government, the British
Government was still responsible for defence, and now
they had to move soldiers in, to keep the two factions
apart and to retain some order in the country. There
were soldiers everywhere. To preach the Gospel under
such conditions meant that we risked our lives every
time we stepped outside the front door.

It could have been suicidal for me, being of Indian
descent, to enter a village where there was a majority of
Africans. It became apparent in this tragic situation that
our mixed marriage had God's design behind it. I was
acceptable to Muriel's people because she was my wife.
She became my passport into their hearts and vice versa.
Bryn and I thought that we should not wait until more
convenient times. If ever there was a right time to come
with the good news of love and peace to the troubled
villages, it was then. Jesus loved these people, and cared
what happened to them.

We introduced ourselves to the churches in the city,
and explained to the leaders that we really wanted to
serve them. We were disappointed though because they
wanted to own us exclusively; and for us to have been
totally identified with one particular group would have
been counter-productive. Harry had already started
work two years before our arrival. Through much
suffering and sacrifice he reached out mainly to Hindus
and Muslims. He was stoned, physically abused and
slandered, but through it all he fearlessly preached the
Gospel of Christ. Through his work, churches were
born. He took Bryn and me on a reconnoitring mission,
and we discovered that while there were many
denominations fighting for their patch of ground in and
around the city, for some reason the missionaries had
not penetrated the countryside. Barely five miles outside
the city, it was difficult to find a living evangelical
witness. We drove for miles, passing village after village,
dusty road after dusty road punctuated by many pot-

holes, crossing river after river, without locating a single committed, born-again Christian.

Clearly it was to the poor people in these run-down, unattractive areas that we must go, braving water-shortages and mosquitoes, driving on dirt roads with burnt earth spread over them. When we returned from a journey, Bryn's blonde hair looked even more blonde, covered as it was with red dust. To negotiate the pot-holes needed considerable skill. But we ventured, in our Volkswagen with the PA system mounted on top.

When we entered a village, we parked the bus and introduced ourselves by visiting the homes. This often gave us an opportunity to pray for people's needs and misfortunes and for the sick. Sometimes we were well received, but often we were rebuffed, insulted and driven out. Whenever it was possible we would conduct open air meetings. Some of these were never-to-be-forgotten experiences. Many people assembled and some outstanding conversions and healings took place.

One warm sunny Saturday afternoon, as we were entering a particular village on the west coast, a young lady who had accepted Christ two weeks before came rushing out to meet us. She was barely four feet tall, plump, with long flowing brown hair and beautiful bright black eyes. Our van was filled with young people from the city, who usually came out with us on Saturdays. The girl was very agitated.

"Please turn back. Don't come into our village today," she said.

"Why?" we inquired.

"I overheard my brothers and a few others planning to kill you today. Please do not come," she said. Communist influence was very strong in these villages, and nationalistic spirit was at fever pitch. It didn't take much to cause a full-scale riot. The message of Jesus was a threat not only to communists, but to Muslims and Hindus as well. We were not coming to friends, we were bringing a message of love and peace to people who regarded us as enemy number one. We knew this. What could I do? I turned the Volks round as I thanked the distressed maiden, and drove away.

I must have gone a mile when I stopped. I was threatened, and what did I do? Run like a frightened chicken! Grasshopper man. I tried to tell myself that I must be wise and not take unnecessary risks. In my mind's eye I saw three lovely girls smiling at me as if they were saying "Daddy". My heart went out to them and to Muriel at home. Bryn and Edna were away in the Corentyne that weekend. Take it easy. Be wise. How often I had prayed, "Lord, I am willing to serve you whatever the cost." Right now I was tempted to forget those prayers. I debated within myself for a few minutes, then I turned to the young people in the minibus and asked them what they thought. All were agreed that we should not give in. Back to the village we went and continued visiting and praying as we had before. Then we gathered in our usual place for an open-air meeting. We sang, and after a testimony from one of the young people, I began to preach, timidly at first, until a strong anointing of the Holy Spirit dispelled my fears.

Suddenly I saw them coming – the men who were intending to kill us. I preached on fearlessly and with a boldness I had hardly experienced before. As they reached the edge of the crowd, they suddenly stopped abruptly and stood there as if arrested – transfixed. With my gaze firmly fixed on them, I continued to appeal for people to accept Jesus as Saviour, and several Hindus responded. The men remained looking distinctly uneasy as we prayed. Then I felt an inner compulsion to go over and speak to them – rough-looking men with violence written all over their faces. I approached them with an outstretched hand which they refused with a piercing look of disdain. Then, after looking me up and down, the leader spoke up, his eyes blazing with hate.

"Who are you?" he blurted out vehemently.

"I am Philip and I love you. What is more important is that Jesus loves you. Jesus really loves you," I repeated, feeling a lot bolder. His countenance changed. Then he related that they really came to kill me. Why? I offended them firstly because as an Indian I had no right to be a Christian, and secondly, because I brought people of African descent in my team to their village. In any case they had their own religion and I preached Jesus and represented Christianity. To them this was a white man's religion, a political gimmick used to exploit and repress the poor. It was an insult to their ideology. They explained that they did not believe in God anyway, but some strange power had arrested them as they came near to our meeting, and that power was restraining them still.

"Jesus loves you, my friends," I replied. With tears of compassion I laid my hands on the shoulder of the leader and said, "May I pray with you?" I knew that the Spirit was working in their hearts. They all bowed their heads. The Gospel of peace came to that village, and a church was founded.

One Sunday morning as we were worshipping in Stanleytown, the father of two Muslim teenage lads who had accepted Jesus went berserk and came rushing in shouting obscenities and chopping the wooden rails with his cutlass as he went. "On your knees everyone, and call on Jesus!" I shouted.

"Jesus, Jesus, in the name of Jesus, the blood of Jesus!" they all responded, one lone voice also crying out: "Satan, the Lord rebuke you!" The two boys, afraid and ashamed, took refuge behind me, but the poor man did not know what hit him. He turned with haste, dropped the well-sharpened blade he was wielding, and ran off as though he was on fire, shouting, "Mercy, mercy", while the villagers who by this time had gathered outside expecting to witness a massacre, were left standing in astonished silence.

One day we were busy with various duties. Bryn and I

were working on a duplicated magazine on the ground floor, Edna and Muriel busy in the kitchen, the children playing in the living room. Suddenly the usual street noises outside were interrupted by a disturbingly loud BANG. The thundering sound sent shock waves through the city streets. The house shook. We thought it would collapse. The traffic outside stopped, the children screamed, Edna and Muriel were in tears. People were running helter-skelter and pandemonium reigned. Bryn and I rushed upstairs to calm our wives and the children, and eventually we learned that a house not far away had been bombed to the ground, a whole family of eight perishing in the blast. It was in this climate of fear, distress and uncertainty that we were seeking to appeal for calm, pointing people to Jesus, the Prince of peace and source of love, often risking our lives to hold forth the message of reconciliation. Here were people with odds stacked heavily against them who seemed to have such deep irreconcilable hurts that they were hell-bent on their own destruction. I realised more than ever before that racial differences, racist attitudes and prejudices were not the monopoly of any one race or culture. They should be identified and repented of.

Bryn and Edna, Harry Das, Muriel and I continued to live and work together as a team. Bryn and Edna in particular used to travel to the Corentyne to help Harry to minister to the young church which had been planted there as a result of his faithful witness over recent years. I continued to lay foundations in the groups which had come to birth since our arrival in the previously unreached villages. In two years, six different churches were planted, scattered over an eighty-mile stretch of countryside divided by the swift flowing Demerara river.

One night I was working very late when at two o'clock in the morning Muriel called, "Phil, come quickly, come quickly!" I burst open our bedroom door, and there stood Muriel with Christine in her arms. Shock was written all over her face; clearly something was seriously wrong. Christine was limp, her neck fallen back: to all intents and purposes, she had died in her mother's arms. She had been suffering for a few days from asthma. She had suffered very serious attacks since we had arrived in Guyana. I looked at her, looked at my wife, and thought, "Oh no, I am sure this is not the Lord's intention." I cradled Christine in my arms – her little body, although still warm, had no pulse, no breathing, was just limp. I summoned up all the faith I could find, lifted up my voice and said: "In the name of Jesus, Christine, come back here!"

A deathly hush ensued. Eternity seemed to be present, time suspended as it were. I actually felt as though from the window across the room, Christine re-entered that limp body, opened her eyes, and began breathing again. It will always be a matter of conjecture whether at that moment she had really died. All I knew was that my daughter was not there, I was holding a corpse. And she came back. That night, God restored our child to us. We knelt down, with tears in our eyes, and offered her back to God. A gift twice given.

During the first months after our arrival when Christine was three years old, Muriel came in from a visit to the doctor and shared some good news. She was pregnant. Number 4 was on the way. In spite of hardship and financial problems we were overjoyed. At last this one must be a boy, we thought. As the pregnancy progressed, Muriel became more and more tired and unwell. She looked larger than would normally be the case. Then to all our surprise after an X-ray it was discovered that she was carrying twins. Oh what a thing! This was not four but five as well! Not one boy but two! We joked and laughed and waited. She could not really manage at home and had to be admitted into hospital a fortnight before.

On 25th April 1965 Muriel almost died on the delivery

table, but after much prayer and much work by the doctors, she presented me with two of the loveliest girls you have ever seen. Identical twins. Muriel was OK for the first two days, only tired. I had to get two of everything. It felt strange but I was a very happy father. On the third day I arrived at the hospital to find that Muriel was in a very deep sleep and her hands had been strapped with the sides of the bed up. I thought it was strange so I sat and waited, content for her to rest. Slowly it dawned on me that something was wrong. I was told that she was suffering from severe post-natal depression. My dear wife suffered such a shock to her system that it took twelve months for her to recover from that ordeal and three years before she was able to resume her normal duties. During those first weeks Edna proved to be a real sister to us. She cooked, washed, tended the children and cared for Muriel with such love and tenderness. She was amazing. We can never repay her for being such a tower of strength and support to us as a family when the chips were down.

CHAPTER FIFTEEN

The team expands

The work expanded, making more and more demands on our meagre finances and energy. Although born and brought up in Guyana, I too was beginning to feel the effect of constant, long hours of labour, and the energy-sapping heat, added to which, there were many days when we had to go without proper meals. It became apparent that if we were to fulfil the vision, we needed to rethink our whole strategy. There is a limit to what three people can accomplish. At the best of times, although we have varying capacities and capabilities, we are limited. We cannot stretch ourselves in an ever-expanding work without suffering the inevitable consequences of re-producing poor quality believers and risking our health in the process. As we prayed about this, I was reminded of Jesus and his disciples: how he chose twelve and spent much time with them, teaching them, eating with them, taking them out as he preached to the multitudes and healed the sick, answered the questions of the Pharisees and travelled around the towns and villages preaching the Kingdom. I was also reminded of Paul, how he had a team, and would disciple other men, ordain them as elders, train them as Timothys and Tituses. That word in Joshua became meaningful and I understood what God was saying to us. It was to raise up other disciples, to train and groom them for leadership.

We were ill-equipped for such a task. The idea of training others to lead the churches that we had pioneered was exciting, but required greater resources than we had ever seen hitherto. However, we began praying that God would confirm his will by sending us people to train. It was just at this time that Ivor Hopkins from Wales, who was a fellow student with Bryn and Edna Jones at the Bible College of Wales, came from Dominica to join us in Guyana.

One day, Bryn and I were sitting in the Volkswagen in Lombard Street in Georgetown, waiting to collect a suit from the tailor, when a young man walked up to the bus and said, "Are you Philip Mohabir?"

"Yes," I said. "Who are you?"

"I am Neville Solomon, from Golden Grove on the east coast," he told us. "I was praying and asking God, what was his purpose for my life. I had grown dissatisfied. I came to know Jesus through the ministry of an Assemblies of God minister. While I was praying about this, I distinctly heard God say to me, "Go to Lombard Street, until you see a white bus. Ask that man – he is Philip Mohabir, and he will tell you what to do."

That was how we had our first Timothy. God added six others in a few weeks and we started training them. The other brothers decided that while they would teach, they assigned to me the solemn responsibility of being in charge of this area of our activity. The students were not very academic, but then neither was I. They were an odd bunch really. None of them had any 'O'-levels, but they were intelligent. They were Indians, Africans, Amerindians, an amazing mixture of all three racial groupings: seven Guyanese, not only different in culture, but in personality as well. I had the job of moulding these men into a team without crushing their own particular individuality or turning them into clones. The challenge for a man barely twenty seven, who himself was only a rugged evangelist, was more than I thought I could handle, but I was determined to try. I realised that the success or failure of our vision and mandate hung on this particular activity.

Muriel and Edna played their part by doing what they could to put something on the table as often as possible. We had no desks, no classroom, no furniture, but I took our students out with me and taught them while we were walking or sitting beneath a tree by the bank of a canal. I sought to teach them partly through real life situations, yet I was careful to teach them also all I knew from the word of God. It was encouraging to see the changes in these young men as they grasped the vision and grew in their understanding of the scriptures. They wanted to get involved even though it meant making sacrifices. They were eager and keen. They went hungry, and often had to walk miles to reach a village; they lived with the uncertainty of not knowing where the next meal was coming from. They gave up promising careers in order to serve. They were daring, bold young men.

Whatever may have been accomplished in Guyana was the work of a team. As well as Harry, Muriel and me, Bryn and Edna, Ivor and Stan and Brenda, we were also joined by two Canadian sisters who spent two years with us. Evelyn Splane and Elizabeth Olmstead will always be remembered for their infectious smiles, fervent prayers, and willingness to attempt the impossible and to be identified with the people. Sydney Bygraves who was originally from Jamaica but had settled in Toronto, Canada, worked over many years with great effect in Vergenoegen; Violet Lewis, a children's evangelist also from Jamaica trained many in children's work. She was one of the most hard working helpers some years later when we were carving out a village in the jungle – of which more later. She and Bernice Morgan, an Arubian of Guyanese parents, were right and left-hand workers in those trying years. Violet and Bernice became a real source of strength and support to Muriel and me. Their greatest asset was their intercession. Violet has the distinction of being the first woman to build her house by her own hands in the village. An inspiration and challenge to the rest.

Our teams were very mixed: black and white, men and women from different church and denominational groups and different cultural backgrounds. There were differences of opinion, different styles of leadership, different approaches to situations and methods of dealing with people. We had different tastes in food. It was Bryn who first taught us to toast a thick slice of bread with cheese, onions and tomatoes on top. He called it Welsh Rarebit or something like that. Instead of dwelling on our differences we pooled our resources, and all our lives were enhanced by the variety.

Apart from the 'ex-patriate team', there is a whole army of national and local men who are the real heroes, among them our original seven students. Neville Solomon I have told you about already. He was of African descent and had been converted as a teenager. He was my first Timothy and a tower of strength when several of our team left for Europe and the USA. A faithful man, he married Maureen, one of seven in the Bruyning family who were among the first converts in Stanleytown. When a call came from St. Martin, he was the best man we could send: the first missionary sent out from our midst.

Kedlall Jhugdeo was of Indian descent and came from a Hindu background. He was converted in the early pioneer days in a remote village called Richmond beside the mighty Essequibo, a river twenty miles wide with three hundred and sixty five islands and hundreds of tributaries, host to one of the world's highest waterfalls – the majestic Kaieteur with a 787 foot perpendicular drop. The meetings at which Kedlall Jhugdeo was converted were conducted by Kanhai, one of Harry's converts. Ked joined us as a rough and ready uncut diamond. He pioneered the Vergenoegen work with his young wife Joyce and went as our first missionary to Surinam to work with James Cooper. Later he co-pastored the church in Georgetown with me for a while. James and Linda Cooper are Americans with whom we have a close bond and working relationship.

Harry Outar, also of Hindu extraction, was one of the fruits of the Saturday open-air meeting in the village where they plotted to kill me. Married to Anjannie, a convert from an island in the Essequibo, he now leads a church in Surinam.

Lucius Bruyning is the second son of the Bruyning household – the first teenage boy to be converted in Stanleytown. He later led several teams on the east coast and pioneered the work in New Amsterdam. He now leads the church in Georgetown.

Malcolm Sobers comes from Buxton, one of the first villages established after slavery by the ex-slaves themselves. He is an outstanding prophetic teacher with an itinerant ministry to the churches, and is married to Anita who hails from Bartica, a convert of Mohammed Yasin who himself was converted from Islam. Mohammed is from my village. He is known as the apostle to the interior where he has pioneered a thriving church with many congregations scattered in the hinterland regions.

Wallace Van Tull leads the church in the neediest and poorest districts of Georgetown, notorious for vice. Many there have been delivered from drug addiction and rejection. He had the faith and vision to build a rehabilitation centre in this area, and has pioneered churches in Mahdia and Arouca River. He is married to Deowatti and they have five beautiful children.

Winston McGowan is a university lecturer, trained in Jamaica and Great Britain. He is married to Maureen who worked in the Ministry of Education.

Ramsaywack Somai leads the team in West Demerara. Frederick Jeffers, originally from Albertown church, was sent out to Mabaruma where he has led six churches in that interior hinterland border town for many years. He is married to Ruby who was my first secretarial assistant. Fred met her while waiting to see me from time to time when he was in Georgetown on business relating to his work. They are doing an excellent job mainly amongst the Amerindians under severe and testing conditions.

Time and space will not permit me to tell you about Deonarine, Elma, Lloyd, Winston, Lennie, Louis, Dinah, Edmund, McCurdy, Cecil, Paul, Elsworth, Joe, Noreen, Ivy, Yvonne, Pansy, Zahoor, Pammy, Doris, Keeshan – our many faithful fellow-labourers and helpers. A whole army of unsung heroes. I pay tribute to them all, especially to our women whose contribution cannot be measured and without whom we could not succeed.

Sherlock and Mavis Tacodeen were our closest friends and supporters in Georgetown in the early pioneer days. Sherlock, who came from a Hindu background in a village on the Essequibo coast, worked hard long hours to serve the church, to supervise a whole building project and to care for my family when I was attending to the Hauraruni village pioneer programme. He is now an elder in the church at Munder in the Paramaribo, Suriname. He is our main printer in the small print shop which is now based in Suriname.

The remarkable thing about this band of people who worked together in Guyana, a country torn at the time by inter-racial feuds, is how mixed we were, both in race, culture and social class. People of African and Indian descent working together in love and harmony in Guyana in the early nineteen sixties and onwards – truly it was a miracle which only God could have achieved.

CHAPTER SIXTEEN

The church grows in Guyana

In autumn 1966, Bryn and Edna felt it was time for them to return to the UK. They encouraged Muriel and me to come with them and to pursue our work as a team but based in Britain, so that together we could implement the plan God had shown us for the cities of England. However, try as I might to free myself from the responsibility for the young men we were training in Guyana, and for the young churches which were emerging there and at different stages of development, I could not. I knew that God wanted me to do something more in Britain. My call to be a missionary in Britain was still alive. Everything inside me responded to the idea. Yes, let's go. After all – Guyana wasn't the centre of the world. Much more could be accomplished if we were in Britain. We could reach many more countries; many more untouched, unreached areas. But I found no peace to walk away from the situation in Guyana and leave for Britain. I realised that I might be closing the door of opportunity and that by remaining I was going to be alone – our best friends would be many miles away. What is more I was exposing my wife and children to more hardship, and asking them to share a less comfortable existence and to go on making sacrifices. When Muriel and I shared with Bryn the way we were thinking, he did not discourage us, but he did not agree with us either. As we parted at the airport, he said:

"I'll be waiting for you on the other side. I am going to

make preparations for you all to join us within three months. Do all you can to tie up loose ends here. See you soon."

Those were our parting words. Bryn boarded the plane and flew away into the clear tropical skies: and as I stood on the tarmac and watched the plane disappear I felt that a part of me had flown away for ever. From then onwards I hardly ever heard from Bryn, but the church in Guyana will always be grateful to him and Edna for the invaluable contribution that they made. Then Harry Das, who was doing a great job in the Corentyne also suddenly announced that God was leading him to pioneer a work in the USA, which would become the base from which he would reach out to many other nations, and he too departed. The team disintegrated. In a few months Ivor, who had been much appreciated for his teaching ministry in Guyana, and who married one of our foremost, dedicated and active young women, also left and now leads a fellowship in Wirral, Merseyside, under Bryn. We were left with twelve churches and these seven young men, and our five children. We were now alone, so we encouraged each other. The wise counsel and support that my wife gave me were never more appreciated than at this time.

The months immediately following their departure were really difficult but the vision was still alive, and we were convinced that our job was not completed. Together we knelt down beside our bed, arms thrown across each other, and rededicated our lives to fulfil all that was in God's heart for us in Guyana and the West Indies. Whatever the cost, we could not turn back. We could not leave the fledgling churches. To leave these young men whom we had encouraged to step out, who had left all their prospects to serve the Lord, seemed not only criminal but a denial of all the Kingdom principles we were seeking to establish among them. It would be a betrayal of their trust. We had no alternative. We stayed.

It was becoming far too expensive for us to keep the house in Georgetown, or indeed to live anywhere in the city. We had to give it up and seek cheaper accommodation. The church in the village of Stanleytown was steadily growing and was the most encouraging prospect for a model and a base, although we would be separated from Georgetown, the capital, by the wide swift-flowing murky Demerara river. But we had no other viable option. The believers there provided us with the best potential for a base, so with their encouragement, we moved to Stanleytown, hiring a small house for the family and something that was little more than a cottage hut for the seven men. Those were real days of adventure. We would wake up in the morning to find everywhere covered with red dust and bat-dung. Rats were running wild everywhere. Cockroaches crept out of every piece of woodwork – thousands of them. Spraying gave temporary relief but never got rid of them. It was difficult to prepare meals on a one-burner kerosene primus stove. Most of the furniture we had in Georgetown had been sold and the proceeds distributed among the various team members to help defray the expenses incurred during the partnership. The lion's share of outstanding financial obligations was left for me to pay off as God would provide.

Obliquely opposite the spot where we conducted our open-air meetings in Stanleytown was where the Chand family lived. He owned a grocery store and a liquor restaurant and a sizeable piece of land at the back of his shop on which he had erected a dance-hall. Since our coming to the village his trade had dropped, partly because of the race-riots and partly because of the impact of the Gospel. Converted people were no longer interested in the drinking, fighting, dancing and other unseemly behaviour that used to go on there. We needed a meeting place for the growing number of believers, so I thought about approaching Mr. Chand with a view to purchasing the land and the building.

"This is real crazy," I thought. "I don't even know if the man wants to sell! And in any case I have no money with which to make such a purchase." I doubted my own sanity. His wife and four of his daughters had accepted Christ, and he was very impressed, although he himself was a professing Hindu, with the changes that had taken place in their lives and attitudes. He was a very kind man, so I thought it could not do any harm if I made him an offer, which I proceeded to do. In response, he politely said that he would see what his wife and children thought about it. After a week, I returned to hear the verdict: "You can have it brother, but how much can you pay me?"

I was taken by surprise as I did not expect quite such a prompt transaction. I had to be honest with Mr. Chand and tell him that I had no money, but wanted the place for the work of God. Could he possibly make an arrangement, and give me a mortgage? Without batting an eyelid, he took me to his lawyers next day, and drew up a document. To the lawyers' consternation, he gave me a full mortgage for that property. We have since paid it off.

That became our first freehold property and gave us a solid base in Guyana. The seven young men and myself, with the help of the believers in the church, set about renovating the hall and extending it to provide a meeting place and a dormitory for the men in training, as well as living accommodation for us as a family. It was a project of faith. Each time I received a few dollars I would purchase a few concrete blocks and a sack of cement. Each time we ran out, the Lord would work a miracle and I would go and get some more. The work progressed unhindered. A few months later, after many long hard hours of work, we were able to move in. It seemed to us a palace in comparison with the conditions we had been living in. Even the children felt as though

Christmas had arrived early. The villagers who had watched us at work were loud in their commendation and held us forth as examples to others. We earned much good will for the Gospel. Stan Wood was a tremendous help, having been a builder before he entered full-time ministry. He and his wife Brenda and their two little boys had come out and joined us from Liverpool at Bryn's invitation soon after the rest of the team left. Stan was a great inspiration to the young men, often going out with them and engaging in pioneer evangelism.

From Tuesday to Friday Muriel and I prayed with and taught the men both in the classroom and in real life situations. They converted the vacant plot beside the building into a vegetable garden. We kept a few chickens. All this helped to supplement our income and to improve our diet. Every weekend, the men and I went out two by two, visiting the churches and pioneering new ones. The roads were terrible. I made it a deliberate policy to take mixed racial teams. We needed to make a prophetic statement and to demonstrate that the Gospel transcends all barriers. Every Friday mid-day we pooled all our pennies together, and distributed them according to need. Sometimes it was not enough to get us more than a few miles away, but some of those men walked for miles to reach their destination. We would return on Monday morning, sometimes very hungry and tired, but with stories of victory, of souls saved and people healed – sometimes persecuted, but happy. It was praise, rejoicing time.

In 1967, I felt that we needed to organise a special annual event for the growing number of young people who were turning to Christ. Consequently a youth arm was launched called 'Guyana Youth Aflame'. A camp meeting in August was the high point of their activity each year. They were encouraged to grow food, and were trained in various skills, occupying themselves in

different arts and crafts. One day at each camp was
dedicated to an exhibition of the things they had done
over the year. The first camp had an attendance of 36,
and within four years it grew to four or five hundred
people. This annual activity became the most significant thing we did during that difficult period of
Guyana's history. Many people turned to God. Many
saw the gifts of the Spirit in operation, and were filled
with the Holy Spirit. In the mornings there were Bible
studies on specific topics relevant to the issues of the
time, in the afternoons there were quizzes and
workshops, and in the evenings celebration meetings
were held.

Many excellent young men and women who are still
in the ministry today, first responded to God's call in our
camp meetings. They had good career prospects but
decided it was better to obey the Lord. You cannot do
better for yourself than by being in the perfect will of the
Lord. Some of them really fought hard and long to resist
the call of God on their lives. There was no human
pressure put on them, it was just a sovereign work of
God, a very manifest work of the Holy Spirit.

Winston Lynch actually stayed as far away from the
meetings as possible, busying himself with the pots and
dishes in the cooking area because he was determined
that God would not get hold of him. All of a sudden, we
heard a rumbling, tumbling, mournful sound from the
nearby bush. It was Winston bawling his head off:

"Yes, Lord, I will Lord, have mercy Lord, I will." His
resistance broken, the love of God overcame him – with
no human involvement. We were caught up in a
wonderful time of worship as with tears, he stood in front
of all three hundred campers, making a total commitment to follow the Lord wherever he might lead.
Winston never once turned back. Today, he is in Kenya
reaping the rewards of such obedience, and the Lamb is
receiving the just reward of his sacrifice. Aubrey came

from the Pomeroon river. He is a mixture of African and Amerindian blood, a young man with tremendous dreams who also met the Lord, in unusual and direct miraculous dealings of the Spirit in the camp meetings. He trained for four years with us, and is now serving the Lord with remarkable success in Jamaica. Lionel Etwaru sat in a corner, lips sealed tight, teeth gritted in a dogged determination not to yield. During the course of the meeting, I glanced over and saw that he was in distress. I thought that perhaps he was sick, that some strange malady had taken hold of him. I grew concerned as I noticed his obvious increasing discomfort and pain. Eventually I went over and asked him if he was OK.

"Leave me alone," he said. Then I realised that God was dealing with him with a very strong hand. Stubbornly he resisted and argued, fixed in his determination not to say yes. Then towards the end of the meeting, he beckoned to a few of us standing nearby.

"Please pray for me. I am paralysed. I cannot move. I have decided to go forward, but I cannot move." A tall, dark and handsome young Indian man, barely nineteen years of age. Four of us lifted him and carried him to the front of the meeting. He prayed, dedicated his life, burnt his bridges behind him, tore away the idols from his heart and surrendered unconditionally to Jesus. His whole countenance changed, his limbs relaxed and a joy unspeakable flowed through his being that infected all who were present in a time of hilarious joy and rejoicing. We did not get to bed till late that night.

Such unusual and unorthodox dealings of the Holy Spirit we witnessed year after year. Many were delivered from bondages and healed, and numerous lives were changed. Couples who could not have children received miracles. Cancers and other chronic illnesses were healed, and demons were cast out. The acid test of time has proven that they were real. The glory belongs to the Lord of Glory, who alone can do mighty things. By adopting the method of apprenticing, reproducing others who could do our work, delegating and sending them out, more churches were born in the various districts that God had indicated in my basement-room vision in Brixton so long ago.

We were still based in Stanleytown. While we were there, our sixth and last daughter, Deborah, was born, three weeks overdue. After the first week my wife was looking drawn and very unwell – she was visibly struggling. I took her across the river to the gynaecologist at the hospital, who just said "Go home and rest." We took lodgings in the city, and two weeks later, very worried by now, I took her to the gynaecologist again, who after examining her sent us away, assuring us that all was well and that the baby would come in due course when it was ready. That night I could not sleep, and at five in the morning the Holy Spirit said to me, "Take Muriel straight to the hospital." Muriel was afraid of being ticked off when we got there, but I was prepared to take the blame and said, "We must obey." As soon as we arrived, the midwife took Muriel in and called the doctor. Deborah was delivered by a Caesarian operation, and I was told that had I waited a few more minutes before bringing Muriel to the hospital, I would have had to bury them both.

Meanwhile the number of people in training increased dramatically, and we had to expand by building more accommodation. With funds so hard to come by and every penny already accounted for, this new venture stretched our faith to its maximum limit. One afternoon in 1968 while I was working with the young men erecting a fence, I collapsed and suffered a minor heart attack. I was receiving clear signals to take things easy, but I was alone and could not really afford to neglect my responsibility to the young men. I felt helpless and also stupid that I was not observing a more sensible life-style. As I lay on my bed I cried out to the

Lord for forgiveness and healing: "God, I cannot give up now. I cannot slack up, the vision is not yet fulfilled."

A few days later I was able to resume my normal duties but this time I realised that I must take necessary precautions. I started to take an hour's siesta in mid-afternoon when the sun was at its hottest. My only transport was a Solex, a motorised cycle, very ill-equipped to handle the muddy roads on which we had to travel. I never want to see one of those Solex bikes again. I pushed that thing a lot more than it carried me. Some weekends I travelled 180 miles on that cycle in order to minister to six churches.

Our friends in Sweden and also our sister Eva Carr in London heard about my illness. Eva contacted the Swedish brothers and together they sent me a ticket to spend first some time in London and then to go on to Sweden. The promise that our Swedish friends had made earlier, to stand with us and to support us regularly, had never really materialised, except from the one faithful brother who had come to us early in the morning in Rorvik, convinced that the Lord was telling him and his wife to support us. Many a month their gift was the only money that we could rely on to keep our family alive, but the Lord provided again and again in miraculous ways.

When I reached London, I spent a few days with Egerton and Eva. It was great to see them again. They were glad to see me but shocked at my appearance. I not only felt sick but must have looked sick. Then after a few days I left for Sweden. Hilding and Karl-Erik met me at the airport and they too were very upset at my appearance. I had lost a lot of weight. Later we gathered in Hilding Fagerberg's home in Taberg with a few others. Together we rejoiced over the many things the Lord had done and shared news about Muriel and the children. At a farewell meeting a few weeks later a hundred of our friends gathered and resolved to launch

Evangelical Guyanamissionen. They pledged there and then to resurrect the whole idea of support for Guyana, so that Muriel and the children would not have to undergo such hardship as we had been experiencing. I was very moved as one by one they came up to express their support and to encourage me.

That evening as I retired to bed still savouring the events of the day, I was suddenly transported in my thoughts to the small village of Stanleytown and wondered how my dear wife and children were. I seemed to hear the twins crying in duet. Oh, how I longed to be with them, and would not have objected if, like Philip of the Acts, I had been translated there and then by the Spirit. The hours drifted slowly as I reminisced over the past four years. I saw the many villages stretched along the two hundred miles of muddy roads from Charity to Corentyne. Village after village with temples, mosques, civil disturbances, poverty and deprivation – all unreached and unevangelised. I could hear the cries of men and women resounding in my heart and reverberating in the air. To my utter amazement, despite the renewed offers of support I had received, a strange conflict seized hold of me. Should I go back? Must I go back? Could I not find an easier and more secure way to work for the Lord? This time I knew a lot more about what sort of cost was involved. But the cry of the unreached masses persisted and touched chords of compassion deep within. I felt ashamed that I even contemplated such thoughts of ease and comfort. I was reminded forcibly of my humanity and fell to my knees surrendering myself again to the task yet to be done. It was there that I received my second commission from the Lord to be a missionary to the Guyanas. Refreshed and renewed I departed for Georgetown via London to recommence the work and press further afield to the regions beyond. After an uneventful flight I returned home to the welcome of our band of workers

and the warmth and love of my darling Muriel and our
daughters. They all seemed as if they had grown six feet
taller and looked lovelier than ever in my eyes. It was
great to be home again.

From that time on, our friends in Sweden regularly
sent us money which we used to keep us mobile, and also
to provide us with basic food for the training
programme, and for travel to different parts of the
country. The churches did contribute, but because we
were working mainly in the deprived and poorer
country villages, there was never much money to give.
Indeed many times it was we who helped the poorer
families of the church.

CHAPTER SEVENTEEN

New directions

After seven years in the villages and towns along the coastlands, it became necessary to return from Stanley town to Georgetown. The city is the centre of communications, business, commerce, trade and education. Many of our young people from the churches in the countryside migrated to the city to pursue higher education and better job opportunities. Because we did not have a church or centre in Georgetown it meant we had virtually no contact with them. They were lost to us, in terms of their involvement and contribution. Some of them represented the best potential for local leadership, and I thought that if the work was to have a future, we needed to retain people of this sort. To ensure perpetuity for the churches and to facilitate the increasing administrative demands, it was imperative to establish a Base Centre in the city. But, to move to the city costs money.

To buy a suitable property to accommodate meetings and offices would be an expensive venture. I was determined this time that I would not rent, because it was like pouring money into a dark hole with nothing to show for it at the end. We prayed for almost a year that God would show us what to do: "Lord, if you want us to move, you must show us where to go." Eventually I woke up one morning conscious of an unusually strong prompting to wait silently and listen. As I prayed and listened, God spoke: "I have a place for you." I actually saw a vision of a colonial type house, large but dilapidated, situated at the corner of two streets.

I was so convinced that God had at last spoken, that I called Ked – one of the more senior men at this time – and shared my heart with him:

"Ked," I said, "I would like you to go to Georgetown today and to approach Mr. X the estate agents. They have a property for sale that would suit us." Ked was as daring as they come. He needed no persuasion; he was the perfect choice for this job. He went off with head lifted high, shoulders square, ready to take the whole of Georgetown apart. That's the sort of man Ked was.

Muriel and I waited anxiously. The shadows were lengthening and the sun sinking fast into the western horizon. Night came quickly; no Ked was in sight. I began to feel anxious, because if he missed the last ferry across the river, it meant he would be stranded for the night. Suddenly, out of the darkness came this towering figure with a broad smile written across his face, and in his deep baritone voice he announced for all in the compound to hear:

"I have found it! I have found it! Praise the Lord!" After the initial excitement and joy he related his story. Through a series of miraculous circumstances he had found the man, who showed him an old colonial house that had belonged to one of the chief justices of our country years ago. It was now in a run-down state needing renovation and refurbishment and for sale for forty thousand dollars. We did not even have as much as four thousand dollars, but we all felt convinced that God was giving us another opportunity to prove him. Next day, Ked and I went to meet the owner, and agreed there and then that we would purchase the house. It was well located, and had possibilities. There was a plot of land alongside it which would give us room for expansion. We managed to muster the 10% deposit, and negotiations began. We were preparing to enter into a whole new development in the work in Guyana.

After a few weeks we were called to conclude the transaction and to pay up the balance that was due. Thirty-six thousand was needed, and not even one thousand in the account. I walked to the Registrar's chambers praying and trusting God with every step, fully believing that by the time our turn came God would intervene on our behalf. Someone, some angel, maybe even a raven, would drop in with that thirty six thousand. One name after another was called. I sat and waited in some excitement, my eyes fixed on the entrance, expecting someone to come in with my miracle. Eventually the proceedings came to an end and our name had not been called, so I approached the Judge, thinking "What an anti-climax!"

"We were summoned today, but we were not called," I said. The Judge asked the clerk to investigate. The man searched everywhere without success. They could not find our papers. The Judge, the clerk and the vendor looked at each other puzzled, but I knew this was no co-incidence. God had intervened in the way I least expected. Another date was fixed for completion, and by the time that date came, the money had arrived: a gift from our brethren in Sweden. So 242 South Street in Georgetown was purchased.

The training centre continued in Stanleytown, but my wife and I felt we should move to the city and pioneer the church there and establish the new base and centre. It was also convenient because by this time our three older girls needed to start secondary school in the city. A small team of helpers moved with us: Pansy and Ruby as secretarial help, and Sherlock – one of the original seven, who served me faithfully in many things and was being trained as a pastor, preacher and printer, and his wife Mavis. After independence, which was gained by Guyana in 1966, I recognised that Christian literature would become more difficult to obtain, and I therefore felt that it was important to have a Christian bookshop and also to seek to print literature locally, with a Caribbean culture and flavour.

We could not really live in the house as it was for very long, so we started to renovate and expand it to accommodate offices, living accommodation for the team, and also a meeting place. We started the church with a nucleus of twelve people, one of whom lived just across the road – a dear lady who had accepted Christ some time before, and was hungry for fellowship. Through prayer and going out to contact people in the surrounding streets, the congregation grew to twenty in a few weeks. Soon Winston Lynch, Ked and Gilbert Martez joined us from Stanleytown. Within eighteen months we were a hundred or more. As the church continued to grow, the ground floor of the house was extended, largely through Brother Ked's leadership, to house six hundred people in the main hall. The church continues to grow, and several other congregations have sprung up in other parts of the city.

The training centre in Stanleytown too became overcrowded. Like the school of prophets in the Book of Kings, the place became too narrow for us. As I waited and prayed I had a vision. I saw that the day would come when Guyana would undergo a very lean period. There would be a scarcity of essential foodstuffs, and there would be political change in the direction of co-operativism. Through a series of co-operative societies, the Government was hoping to restructure the economy of the country. I realised that largely because of the ideology that they had embraced, it would be almost impossible to function without pressure as a traditional church. There were problems ahead which could not be ignored and demanded a solution.

As I waited for direction, I felt God telling me: "Go and ask the Government for a plot of land, and build a village which will become the home and centre of operations in the country. Organise it along the lines of a co-operative. Have not only spiritual activity as such, but also agricultural programmes, industry, manufacturing, and mechanics and welding." As I waited further on the Lord, he explained to me little by little that through this operation we would purchase a lot of good will for the work of the Kingdom, which would enable us to continue preaching the Gospel. This place would be of prophetic significance to the nation and to the regions round about. It would provide a home and security for two hundred or more people and their children – people who had given up all to serve the Lord in various fields without any financial security. If anything should happen to them in the future, this was God's way of providing them with a home, a place with which to identify, a place where they could be trained and sent out, and a place to which they could always return.

Also this operation would demonstrate to the authorities and the powers that be, that the church was not just concerned about preaching for the soul, but for the social welfare and development of the total human being. It was to be a serious attempt to demonstrate the wholeness of Gospel salvation, a holistic approach to the Gospel. This was the largest project I had ever been asked to attempt. I had been in many situations before where my faith was challenged and stretched. Number 23 Dulwich Road, the properties in Stanleytown and Georgetown and several others were all daring ventures of faith: all attempting the seemingly impossible, and God had never failed me. The daily challenge to provide food and other necessities and meeting the running costs of this young work was a continuous adventure of trust in God. We were not aliens to the miraculous. We had witnessed miracles of healing, demons cast out, lives changed, but none more precious to us than the supernatural provision of food and funds to sustain body and soul and keep the bills paid. This sort of thing:

"Phil, we've got nothing to give the children or the workers tomorrow (we were about thirty at this time). What shall we do this time, darling?" enquired my wife with more than a little anxiety in her voice. We were both tired after a long day. I could feel the panic rising in me. "Let's kneel down and pray. It's the only thing we can do." We prayed together, kneeling on the hard wooden floor by our bed like two little kids lost in the woods and then went to bed and sank into a deep sleep, too weary to worry.

At five next morning we were wakened by someone knocking at the door. Mangal, one of the faithful brothers in the Stanleytown fellowship, was standing there with a basket full of *roti* – Indian bread – and a pot of stew: "My wife woke at three o'clock this morning. She couldn't sleep. She felt God saying to her, 'Get up and prepare breakfast for the people at the mission centre.' Here it is. I hope you don't feel insulted," he said half-apologetically. God heard our prayers, and once again graciously, miraculously provided. On another occasion as we sat praying round an empty table laid only with plates and cups, a Hindu lady knocked. Her daughter had accepted Christ a few months before, and she was on her way to the market with a basket of fruit perched delicately on her head. She was convinced that God spoke to her as she passed, saying, "Go and give the fruit to the people at the centre instead." Puzzled, she did so, and as I distributed it, the last one was left in my own hand. One fruit for each of us round the table. God, marvellous and wonderful. Not long after, that lady accepted Christ. Later that evening, someone else came with rice and other groceries so that we were able to cook a proper meal.

But now this vision. I was pygmied by the sheer size and cost of the project. Alarm bells went off in my head; danger signals appeared everywhere. This was not a straightforward Gospel preaching church planting exercise. There were added dimensions with educational, economic, social and political undertones; responsibilities for people's lives. This was an entirely new arena. It could even be a diversion strategy of the Devil to detract from the main burden of my calling which is to build the church. I thought and prayed much. I wanted to be sure that this was God speaking and not just the pressures of the need to expand, pushing my own feebleness to the brink of insanity. First I shared my thoughts with Muriel, thinking this time she really might object. "Phil," she replied, "I have known you long enough now to have decided that if God is leading you, I will stand beside you and support you." I then unburdened my heart to the other leaders – twenty of them, still rather young at the time. They felt a rise of faith and assurance that we should proceed, as did our other full-time workers. So we applied and obtained 460 acres of land from the Government, thirty-five miles from Georgetown on the New Linden Highway linking Georgetown with Linden, the bauxite mining town.

CHAPTER EIGHTEEN

Hauraruni village

So, in 1976, there was an exodus from Stanleytown: seventy to eighty of us with cases, bags, foam mattresses, making our way across the Demerara river in a small launch in the direction of the airport, and then a seven-mile trek on from there to a small clearing in the jungle. It was daybreak when we started. The golden rays of the sun barely penetrated the early morning mist as that great big yellow ball lazily climbed the eastern sky, dispelling darkness, spreading light in its path and heralding a new day. Soft night dew lay on the mangrove trees by the river and on the endless fields of sugar cane and grass. Already at dawn there was much activity: man and beast, bicycles, tractors and trucks travelling on the long dusty road leading to the wooden landing stage where we boarded the launch.

We had had to cut a trail beforehand in order to get through to our chosen site. We had some cutlasses and axes, and a couple of chainsaws, not much more. We cleared that Tarzan-like jungle and made ourselves temporary tents out of branches. We must have looked like a set of simpletons. When the rain fell it went right through. Many times we were drenched, but we were excited. We were on a new venture, and we were building something which we believed God would use one day for his own glory. Little by little we cleared the jungle. Our women folk used the white sand of the area, mixed with cement, to make building blocks for the outer walls of our houses; the trees, after shaving off the bark, were used for door-posts and rafters.

Later, through the auspices of Tear Fund, and through the generosity of our brothers in Sweden, we obtained a sawmill and a tractor. Three brothers from Sweden came to install the mill and to instruct us how to use and maintain it. We were then able to convert the trees into boards, which we used to build simple furniture and pens for our livestock. The village began to take shape, and today is still in the process of being built. It now functions as the base and centre of our work. Here we have camps, conferences, leadership seminars. There is industrial, educational and mechanical activity. There is also an agricultural project for growing local foods – bananas, maize, melons etc. There is now a furniture factory, some of the furniture being sold on the open market, a welding shop, a sewing factory, a primary school, a dental and general clinic, the beginnings of a small library, and a home to accommodate twenty needy children. In the missionary training section, there is room to accommodate ninety six residents. In addition there are twenty-five family units, and thirty or more families are actually resident in the village. We were compelled to cease our poultry farming and the piggery, and to curtail our dairy farming because of the difficulty of acquiring government supplies of feed and necessary medicines.

To pay an occasional visit to dense tropical jungle away from the security of civilisation can be great fun, but actually to carve out a village and settle there can be quite a daunting and frightening experience. It is the sort of pioneer work which summons only the brave or foolhardy. But there are compensations. The jungle abounds with flora and fauna. Orchids and ferns of various kinds blend in with trees twenty metres or more in height, towering over all else as though reaching for the skies and stretching for miles in every direction. The luxuriant and prolific undergrowth provides home and cover for wild animals such as tiger cats, jaguar, sloth, rodents and wild pigs. There are different species of lizard, some just tiny and a few inches long, others monstrous and dangerous things; millions of ants and bees; a paradise of birds and flowers of varying hue and size. The kaleidoscope of colours is rich and fascinating. Incandescent coloured butterflies flit around apparently aimless and unconcerned, a real delight to behold. The denseness of this forest also harbours snakes, some of them large and long and very poisonous and deadly.

One midday I sat very comfortably, some distance away from the hut, in a crudely built outhouse which served as a latrine. It was very hot and sticky. It was a brief but welcome respite from the heat of the sun and constant activity. As I was relieving myself and totally lost in meditation, as one tends to be on these occasions, I became conscious that I was locked in with one of those poisonous snakes. It was staring me in the eyes, flicking its fangs in and out in a very threatening manner. Just three feet away its beady eyes fixed resolutely on me as if to hypnotise me. I could feel the panic rising. Then from somewhere I remembered the words of Jesus, "These signs shall follow them that believe. In my name shall they cast out devils. They shall speak with new tongues, they shall take up serpents, and if they drink any deadly thing it shall not hurt them. They shall lay hands on the sick and they shall recover." (Mark 16: 17–18)

I had cast out devils, seen the sick healed and experienced the new tongues, but serpents? Can it also work with a great big snake ready to attack me? Well, I could not lose. I had only one choice. Sit there a helpless victim or give that old serpent a dose of the Word. So I quoted the Word slowly and deliberately to that snake and it was amazing to see how that creature retreated, eyes still fixed on me, and crawled back into the jungle. I watched and waited until I felt it was out of harm's way, and leapt out of that cubicle, not paying much attention to the state of my decency. Afterwards I reflected how strange it was that some scholars insist that verses 17 and 18 are not part of the inspired word. Well my friends, theology or not, what really matters is that it works.

That village stands as a testimony to the hard work of many young people who made invaluable contributions. There is a lot more yet to be fulfilled, as we continue to develop the original vision. From that base, we have people who are now working in Trinidad, Tobago, St. Lucia, Dominica, Barbados, Aruba, Curaçao, St. Martin and Jamaica. Also, from that base we have sent out young Guyanese couples who are still maintaining those areas of work started years ago in Guyana, as well as seeking to expand into the villages around.

The work was never without its difficulties – financial, of course, but also personality clashes and differences of opinion which were inevitable. But the greatest difficulty appeared just when the whole project was set to climb into higher gear. Some brothers from England visited us, who were witnessing some great and powerful events there. I was happy to welcome them as the burden of all my responsibilities was beginning to weigh me down. Oh, how I needed real brothers to stand by and encourage me, to help me at that time. So I was thrilled when these men arrived. Unfortunately, they came with their own preconceived ideas, and managed to sow seeds of doubt in the hearts of some of my key workers: doubts about my leadership and vision. I was open to hear God speaking through them, and even felt that they were bringing a valuable corrective word into our situation. After all, none of us is infallible. The possibility that I was making mistakes and needing to catch up with what God was doing in the wider world scene was something for which I had always allowed.

It was not until their departure that real problems began to surface with some of the men. They suddenly felt they had received a superior revelation. Unknown to me the English brothers had actively encouraged a few of our men to take hold of the leadership and initiate radical changes – changes which involved the imposition of a culture alien to our particular context. As we tried to discuss the problems in an effort to resolve them and find a way forward, tempers flared and hurts floated to the surface. I could not believe what was happening to the family. It was incredible. Tears, confusion, bewilderment increased as the wranglings dragged on and on. My own lack of confidence and indecisiveness contributed to the insecurity which many felt. Men were threatening to leave, and some had already left. Eventually I realised that there was only one way to pull the whole thing together, and to save it from utter disaster. I called a meeting of the entire fellowship of workers, and declared clearly and simply again what the vision was, what I felt God's direction was for us, my understanding of God's way of government for churches, and the way we ought to be proceeding. I asked them to respond in the light of this. If they were not in agreement, then we should part as friends without any hard feelings, for we could not continue to work in an environment of disharmony, struggle and conflict. That proved to be God's word of wisdom, and from that day we were able to rescue the situation and to continue to build upon the commitment that was renewed. However it must be said that irreparable damage had been done to relationships between brothers and sisters. There was a loss of trust which up to this day has not been fully restored. Also our momentum for growth was lost, and it has taken several years to rebuild the links and begin to regain equilibrium.

The work in Guyana has seen a hundred or more churches come to birth, and although all did not remain under our leadership, sixty six remain and they are a living testimony to what God can do when we dare to obey his call: simple men daring to believe that what God says, he means, and that they that trust in the Lord shall not be put to shame. If someone were to ask what methods we employed to see all of this come to pass, my simple answer would be as follows:

1 Have faith in God to do the impossible

2 Proclaim fearlessly and boldly the essence of the Gospel – a Christ-centred, Cross-centred, Word-based message

3 Be willing to work hard and long, and to make necessary sacrifices

4 Be willing to travail and intercede with fasting and prayer when necessary. Without travail, there is no birth

5 Allow men and women to emerge and grow as Christians without feeling insecure or threatened

6 'Reproduce' as Paul did. If we save our lives, we lose them. If we lose them, we find them again. This is the art of being able to produce other leaders, and so multiply yourself. To produce Timothys by apprenticing people.

7 Never be afraid to delegate and to give away. A missionary's job is never really finished until he has raised up others to take his place. Never become the cork in the bottle. Delegation, however, is not abandonment of your responsibility, but a willingness to share it with others. Delegation without proper accountability is not delegation based on the Bible and does not work in the long run. Accountability however is not holding on to dominant control or the exercise of authority that is dictatorial. Sweet reasonableness is needed.

Another lesson I have learnt is the need to be willing to trust people: have faith in God, but also in your fellow men. Or to put it even better, have faith in God for your fellow men.

Also essential is depending on God to help you to cope with the disappointments of being let down, being attacked, being opposed from the most unexpected quarters and even from those you love. To nurse resentments or to become bitter is a luxury none can afford in the work of the Lord – it is to flirt with disaster and defeat. To go on loving your brethren, whatever their mistakes, is victory. It will certainly involve dying and embracing the cross, but this is the price you pay to ensure that you are still on God's side. We must not have too short a cut-off point. We are working with people. They are unpredictable; they are awkward. We should never give up on them or write them off too hastily. God sometimes finds real pearls and gems in the most unlikely people.

The sixty-six churches for which we have responsibility are composed of mixed races – Africans, Indians, Amerindians; all three major groupings of Guyana. They interact and intermingle at grass-roots and at leadership levels. In the society as a whole, the deep racial divisions that emerged during the years prior to independence are still visible. When people come to Christ, we have to show them the need to face up to their own cultural and racial prejudices, class differences and political allegiances. We do not ask them to deny who they are or to disown their own backgrounds, but it is important that they recognise that now in the Body of Christ, there are no barriers and can be no prejudices. The call is to transcend all divisions by the love of Christ and to learn to accept one another as Christ accepted us. Intermarriage is accepted, because as a new humanity, we do not see anything in Scripture to forbid it. Whenever racial tension arose, we sought to trace the source and then to counsel the people on their own personal problems, helping them to get the victory. Then we would put them in situations where they had to build up the necessary relationships. We would also encourage people to confront each other and share their hearts with one another. On more than one occasion, I have seen how after sharing, they repent, and with tears in their eyes ask each other for forgiveness and start a new chapter together. We would give teaching from Scripture on racial relationships as seen in the eyes of Jesus, and also encouraged people to learn from one another: to develop a better understanding and learn about each other's backgrounds, in order to discover how the other 'ticked', as it were.

In 1965, we preached in two villages just a mile apart, one predominantly Hindu, the other African and Roman Catholic. Fierce animosity raged between the two. When people responded to Christ in both villages, it seemed ridiculous to have two churches, one Indian and one African. I identified the leaders of each section, brought them together and explained that in Christ, we were all new creation people. (2 Corinthians 5:17) "The old has gone, the new has come!" I challenged them to face up to their own attitudes, repent of them and trust the Holy Spirit to give them the mind of Christ. It was touching to see these new converts open their hearts and share their deep inner fears and suspicions – to draw out as it were, from their deep inner selves, the images about each other that had been ingrained in them since childhood.

All was not finished in one session; it took many months. We also organised social gatherings where they could mix and interact and learn from each other as human beings. This worked like magic because they soon realised once they got to know each other that they were not so different after all. They were people with dreams and aspirations and emotions like everyone else. I suppose the greatest contributing factor to this victory were the times of prayer together where people confessed their prejudices and asked God for help – crying out for God to change them, and he did.

In the conferences and camps, we would always seek to

mix the races up so that in every context they worked out their attitudes to one another. In all these situations we stressed the need to respect each other's cultures and backgrounds, not to put pressure on anyone to change what was valuable and good within their own culture. The only pressure for change must be based on the Word, and prompted by conviction by the Holy Spirit, over things that were hindrances to the unity and harmony of the Body. With God's help, they had to work out themselves goals that were for the good of everyone. Often the women got the hang of it first, and then they were able to help the men.

There were times in the pioneer days when it was necessary for the safety of our people, to send Africans to predominantly African villages and Indians to the Indians. But as soon as we had broken the ground in the area, we would mix the teams up. Actually, among the full-time working groups, it was our deliberate policy to mix the races together, thus creating a context in which they had to cope. Often I was called in to sit down with the teams and make peace. I remember the team in Essequibo. There were six of them. The Indian brothers could not really cope with the style and manner of those of African descent; the African contingent could not cope with the Indians. The Amerindians were caught in the middle like the meat in a sandwich. It was not a case of doctrinal differences. It was a simple thing like what food to cook, who should do what chores, how do you address each other. As they talked and prayed and shared, a foundation for better understanding in the team was laid.

I do not presume to claim total success. The process still continues and I am sure there are instances of lingering deep-rooted prejudices. But I am satisfied that when the difficulty is not swept under the carpet, when we do open up and allow God to help us, he does so. Hasten the day, O Lord, when we can all say with sincere hearts that we love without hypocrisy...

CHAPTER NINETEEN

Hard decisions

"I have seen your tears and I understand the burdens of your heart, but I say unto you my son, your work here is finished; you can better serve your brethren outside this situation." This was a prophecy given me in 1981 by an American brother who was part of a party conducting a leaders' seminar in Georgetown. I was attending the seminar with my right leg in plaster because of an injury I had sustained in a car accident a few weeks before. The man knew nothing about me. He had never seen or heard of me before. He made a beeline for me from the platform straight to the back of the hall filled with four hundred or so people. I thought the prophecy very strange, because I was fairly·confident that Guyana was now my base for life. My future life's work seemed to be cut out: to stick with my brethren here, to encourage them, to be a steadying influence and to strengthen their hands. It was an ongoing responsibility. And Guyana as I saw it was to provide resources to launch and develop other areas of ministry and outreach: a base from which to reach into other parts of the world. However I received the word and hid it in my heart as Mary did. When I came home I shared it with Muriel. We prayed and left it in God's hands. We could not see how such a thing could be possible at this stage, but we have learnt that prophesies are not to be despised.

Also in 1981, Muriel became very ill. Brothers in England and in Sweden invited her to convalesce in

Europe. They undertook to pay all expenses, including the cost of return tickets for us both. They planned an itinerary for me in England and Sweden. Muriel stayed most of the time with Dave and Pat Tomlinson. When it was possible she travelled with me. Dave, whom Bryn had sent out to us in Guyana three years before, had ministered among us with great blessing. He was involved with a ministry called Supplyline, which aimed to give material and spiritual support to needy national churches. He was accepted among us as a man who brought much of God's heart to us. He invited me to speak in a ministers' get-together in Newcastle. After that meeting he said to me as I was getting into the car for the ferry to take me to Sweden, "Philip, God has spoken to me to tell you that your time in Guyana is finished. It is time for you to return to England." I was astonished. Could God be confirming the prophecy I had already received? Again, I left it in his hands.

In Sweden, three other such things came spontaneously, right out of the blue, from people who didn't really know of the other things that were said. I then began to pray seriously about God's intention in all this. I could no longer afford to ignore it. It was very difficult to come to a decision, because the implications involved in such a move were too many to contemplate. It would signal a change in our whole approach and direction for the future. As I thought about all this, I was reminded of my early call to be a missionary to England. The idea that the time in Guyana and the West Indies was only for a certain period was renewed. As Muriel and I travelled back to Guyana having spent three months in Britain and Sweden, it became more and more difficult to know what to do next.

Many things had to be considered: practical things like accommodation. We could not afford to buy a bean bag, let alone a house. There were eight in our family. How would we obtain visas – that was practically impossible. In any case, where would we find the money for tickets for eight people? It seemed a discouraging prospect.

Then one day we received a letter from Dave, saying, "We (meaning his team) feel strongly that you should come. Should you decide, we will pay for your tickets and sponsor you into this country. What is more, we have a house dedicated to 'Supplyline' ministry, which is now empty, we shall renovate it and prepare it for the use of your family." In one stroke accommodation, ticket and visa were sorted out without our having to lift a finger. However this decision could not be made without due consideration being given to the repercussions that such a move would have upon the entire work. Guyana was undergoing a time of hardship. Its economy was suffering, and it was tottering on the very edge of bankruptcy, like so many other third world countries that have suffered as a result of world recession. There was scarcity and hardship everywhere. Essential basic foodstuffs were hard to obtain. A loaf of bread could cost up to £2.50, if and when you could get it; a five pound tin of dried milk, £10. For the church leader to depart in such circumstances to a country where there is plenty would be an almost unpardonable sin, a slap in the face of those who trusted us; like the shepherd abandoning his sheep to be devoured. I could not see myself doing it. I wanted with all my heart to stick with my people.

At this time many other preachers and Christians were migrating to Canada, to the USA, to Surinam, and to various West Indian islands looking for greener pastures and golden opportunities for themselves and their families. This was having a serious negative effect on those who remained. Some of them saw it as a serious breach of covenant and commitment, and now I was thinking of doing what looked like the same thing. How could I hope to explain it to them? How could I tell a mother with hungry children that I was going because God had told me to? Would she understand? Would not the other leaders feel that I was abandoning them? Could I really bear the shame and insinuations that our critics would level against me and my family? The struggle went on for several weeks. Muriel and I prayed, but found no real peace to stay, no joy to leave. We were troubled. I wept many tears but waited silently.

We had been married for twenty-three years, but in all that time we had never had a home of our own – always an open house, shared with others; the centre of the work. We don't regret it, but just recently, through the generosity of some brothers in Sweden, a gift had been sent to build a house for my family, here in Guyana. A dear brother by the name of Cornelius Rabess had felt that God wanted him to build it for us. If the Lord gave a house, he must mean us to stay. We had just moved into the house when all of this began to happen – our first little cottage belonging to the family. The pressure increased as the Holy Spirit continued to deal with me. I began to search my own heart for wrong motives. Was I not wanting to let go of the work? Did I not trust the men whom I had trained as leaders to carry it on? Was I interfering with God's ownership? I was sure that this was not the case. It was possible, though, that I could become the cork in the bottle, preventing others from developing their true potential and finding their true level in God. As long as I was there I ran the danger of stifling their development. On the other hand the thought haunted me night and day that I was betraying my people, leaving them in their hour of need. It hurt so much that I just didn't want to hear or know. I just wanted to stay by their side.

In June 1982 we decided as a family that we would all seek God for a definite Rhema word into the situation. (*Rhema* is a Greek word which describes a word from Scripture which is applicable to a specific situation.)

Early one morning, while the birds were still singing in the trees, I locked myself up in my study and fervently asked God to speak so clearly, as he did in times past, that I would be in no doubt as to his commission and heart's desire. As I prayed and waited, this word from Micah 2:10 came with such force and such peace – an unmistakable word for me from God: "Arise and depart, for this is not your (place of) rest." This word told me three specific things: Arise – out of your confusion, your dilemma and your fears; Depart – a clear command; This is not your place of rest – this is not your base forever. That word knocked down all my arguments. I did not have the heart to argue with my Father any more. He had spoken, and as at many other times, he confirmed that with an overwhelming sense of his presence. It was unmistakable. Jesus had come again, to redirect my course. I was melted. I wept, partly because of the joy of hearing clearly at last what he was saying, and partly because I felt ashamed that after all these years I was so slow to hear and to understand.

At the same time, the Lord was confirming this to my wife and children in different ways. It was a big wrench for the children. For the first time, they had a home. All their friends were in Guyana. Two of them were already involved full-time in the work. It meant disturbing the education of the other three. Each of the older children was given the freedom to choose whether to leave or not. No pressure was put on them because we recognised that each was an individual before God and they had their own lives to live. They were all ready to step out into the unknown, but none was as touching as our daughter Anne, who had just met the young man of her dreams after a bitter disappointment a year or so before. How would it work out? She was counting the cost. She felt God wanted her to go, but how could she leave David behind? Would they ever get married, or would this be the end of the road for them? They acted very maturely.

They prayed, and decided that there was only one thing to-do. Obey God now, and trust him to work things out for the future. Later on Anne shared with me that God had spoken to her through the same verse of Scripture as he had used with me – Micah 2:10.

The next thing was to share our decision with the leaders, and I felt that this would be my toughest battle. Dave Tomlinson was present with us for a conference, and I asked him to sit in with us for moral support, and to verify if needed, that God had spoken to him as well. But that was not necessary. God had been preparing my brothers and sisters. As a matter of fact, if I did not know them better, I would have thought that they were trying to get rid of me. But there was no such thing. There was an awe, a sense of God's presence. It was one of the loveliest times of intimate fellowship that we shared as we looked each other in the eye and realised that a major separation was going to take place for which we were not really prepared. One by one however, the brothers shared how God had been speaking to them as he had to me, but they had not fully understood what he was saying. Some did not even want to consider the possibility. One had a dream, the other had a word of knowledge, another a word of prophecy – all with none of us knowing what God was saying to the other. It was like the pieces of a jig-saw puzzle fitting together. Then Dave shared what God had showed to him. So with many tears but with great confidence, we threw our arms around each other's shoulders as we stood in a ring and committed the whole move to God. I sensed in a very real way, a sending forth of my brothers from that moment.

So it was, after many farewell visits to various believers and churches, that in February we boarded a plane bound for England as missionaries – the land from which I had come in 1964. As we settled into the plane, we could still hear the singing and see the tears on the faces of the hundred and more brothers and sisters, the leaders we were leaving behind. The whole Hauraruni village had gathered at the airport to send us off, and as we attended to the practical details of luggage, seat belts and so on with tears flowing down our own cheeks, the strains of 'Our God reigns' and 'Let there be love shared among us' were still ringing in our ears.

CHAPTER TWENTY

England twenty years on

Eventually we arrived in Middlesbrough, England, and were taken to 23, the Avenue, Linthorpe – Supplyline House. It looked empty and quiet but as we opened the door a chorus of "Welcome" burst out from our brothers and sisters in the fellowship at Middlesbrough who had come to greet us. The welcome was warm and loving and kind. It was as though we had moved from one family to another. We felt loved, welcomed and accepted. The brethren, realising we had had a long journey, soon left us alone as a family. When they had all gone, we gathered in the sitting room and spontaneously burst into tears at the love and kindness of our friends who had worked hard to decorate each room with such thoughtfulness. They had furnished them too, with curtains, bed-linen, a well-stocked kitchen with food in the cupboard – even a television! The thing that broke us most was a whole heap of things wrapped in gift-paper in a corner of the room. It was as though we were coming home to Christmas. As we opened up these gifts, things that we needed were there, donated with much love from our brethren in the various fellowships related to Dave's team, including the promise of a car. We wept and we danced, we rejoiced. Eventually too tired to do much else we rolled into warm beds and slept for hours.

It took a few weeks to get settled and adjusted to the pattern and pace of life in Britain. It is such a different world. Then we had to get the children settled in school.

Initially we found it very difficult to go as a family to the shopping centres. There were so many consumer items. Even when we struggled through to buy certain things and bring them home, as we sat down to eat we felt a sadness that we could not share all the good things with those we had left behind. It was hard to come to terms with our consciences on the matter. God had to minister to us. We realised that to gather them all round the table here was a practical impossibility. The important thing was to keep loving and serving our brethren and sharing our life with them, even though it would of necessity be in quite a different way. We needed to ensure that we were not closing our hearts of compassion, unwilling to share what we had, or forgetting them and closing the door on them.

The prophecy which came to me in Georgetown had said, "You could better serve your brethren from outside." What did this mean? We concluded that one way in which we could do this was to interest others in sharing their resources with those at home in Guyana. So, through the auspices of Supplyline, we shared the need with the various churches and began sending food-parcels and in some cases money; where possible we tried to help them with capital and tools to help themselves. The work of Supplyline was at this time, the early nineteen eighties, at its lowest ebb, not having functioned for two or three years. It was difficult to resurrect the whole idea but after a while people began to regain confidence, its credibility built up again, and money came in to launch self-help projects and ministry trips from Britain to third world nations and, on a more short-term basis, to send out immediate relief in the form of boxes of clothing, dried milk and other food items to Christians in Guyana and other needy countries.

Apart from refloating the work of Supplyline, I needed to know what God had brought me back to

Britain to do. At first I welcomed the empty days to relax and rest, for we had not had any proper holiday for twenty years, but soon it was becoming difficult for me to live in the vacuum. I felt dispossessed of my team and somewhat lost for purpose and specific direction. Dave and his team very kindly left it very much up to me: what I would like to do was for me to decide. They made it clear from the beginning that I was under no obligation to the team. However, I felt knitted to them and wanted to get involved. The door was open. Dave was very kind and took me on his many travels. He introduced me to the various churches and leaders. I also made contact with some of my former friends and colleagues. After six months I was beginning to feel introduced and initiated again into the evangelical scene in Britain.

So much had changed since 1956, some of which was a real shock to the system. We did experience culture shock those first few months. Courtesy and politeness seemed to have gone out of society. People were a lot more hostile and aggressive. Standards and morals had declined. The education system had been infiltrated by godless, humanistic philosophies. The Bible was no longer received. Even in so-called Christian circles, the authenticity and authority of the word of God was not fully accepted. So much had changed. Also I was very disappointed to find that some of the men I had known and loved, who were pioneers in renewal and architects and agents for restoring Kingdom concepts to the church, now found themselves in serious tension to the point where they were no longer able to work together. They appeared to have become grounded on the rocks of misunderstanding, broken relationships and personal ambition. It was lamentable; a very sad commentary, and just went to show that history teaches us nothing. These were men I knew, who had worked together in the early days. God had accomplished so much through them in changing church life in this country. This became a matter of great distress to me. I suggested meeting and trying to resolve the issues, but recognised that I did not have sufficient stature among them to influence them, and so I retreated. However I continue to pray for them and keep my heart open to all of them, still nourishing a secret desire that one day there would be harmonious co-existence again, working towards the same goal, building the church, expanding the Kingdom ... In the meantime the people of St. Aidan's Fellowship in Middlesbrough visited us, invited us into their homes, looked after us. They really cared. It was the kind of Christianity that made you feel proud to be identified as a Christian.

As the weeks sped by, things began to crystallise in my thoughts. I felt I should visit our friends Eva and Egerton Carr, who had been our faithful supporters throughout the years. My idea was to go and try to research and assess what was the state of play in and around Brixton. I discovered at once that many black churches were now planted right across London: the network which had come into being while we were still back in Britain had grown. As we explored the scene and investigated, three things became very evident – three major changes which had taken place in Britain during the last twenty years:

Firstly we observed the incredible departure from God and decline of the church, and the continuing decay of morals. A million and a half people had ceased going to church during the past ten years. We saw the rise and prominence of abortion, homosexuality, lesbianism. We observed the battle between the extreme right and the extreme left, the increase of discriminatory practices and injustices, the deprivation, the unemployment, the housing situation, the millions of people living on supplementary benefit. There was the rising rate of crime and the riots of recent years in different cities in

Britain. These things stared us in the face, and made us aware that this was a different Britain. Inner cities had changed. We knew there were problems but never dreamt that they had compounded so many times over. Now there is tension in society, even open hatred. There are militant factions, the escalation of drug abuse, the deterioration of discipline in our schools, the single parent situation. All these things constituted a challenge that was staggering.

Secondly we observed the changing face of British evangelicalism. As we travelled around, and became acquainted with the various church set-ups, it was obvious that much had changed in the churches. Although the orthodox more well-known churches were losing their membership at an alarming rate, there was a change of climate in many of the evangelical churches: greater freedom of worship, a greater sense of expectancy, an acceptance of the miraculous and supernatural. Obviously something had happened. The charismatic outpouring of the Holy Spirit had brought renewal, so the same congregations that would have been cold, dull and boring would now sing to guitar music, clap their hands and even play tambourines! Those were things that only West Indian churches did when we were here. Now people would raise their hands in the air and clap and even dance. English white, evangelical Christians dancing and clapping their hands, and praising God! That in itself is a miracle that we West Indian Christians never thought would happen. After all, anyone who indulged in such spontaneous expression of their emotions in worship would earlier have been considered an exhibitionist, improper and irreverent.

The other positive thing about the changing face of British evangelicalism is that Christians have become more aware of their responsibility to get their hands dirty and to be involved in social action. They see the need to relate to people's actual needs: not only to preach the Gospel for the soul, but to present a holistic message for the whole man. They have begun to reset their agendas to meet and deal with contemporary issues as they relate to modern man. It was also obvious that they had opened up to the supernatural gifts of the Holy Spirit, speaking in tongues, prophesying, words of knowledge, praying for the sick. What is more, they were seeing results! New churches were planted, hundreds of them, meeting in school buildings and community centres. These are often referred to as House Churches.

Thirdly we were amazed by the phenomenal growth of the black-led churches in this country over the last twenty to thirty years, so that it is claimed by some that there are now three thousand or more such churches scattered throughout the major cities of Great Britain. However, the tragic fact is that while the traditional, white evangelical churches had been renewed, and new churches were being born at an encouraging rate throughout the country; and while there was on the other hand a phenomenal growth in the black evangelical, pentecostal churches, these two most dynamic groups of God's people in this country hardly mixed and seemed largely unaware of each other's existence. There was a quiet, subtle system of apartheid operating in Great Britain's churches. The British Council of Churches, for example, had very few black members within its ranks, and very few if any within its council of management. The Evangelical Alliance in 1983 had two black individuals as members, and one registered black church. Even where there are mixed congregations, their leadership does not reflect the mix of black and white Christians. Black leaders and their churches hardly if ever have an opportunity to share or contribute into the wider evangelical family. For some reason or other, they are denied the joy of working in any meaningful partnership with their white counter-parts. To them it is a closed constituency. In twenty years the two groups had not grown any closer to each other. Preferences had become prejudices and over the years these prejudices had hardened.

As I continued my investigation, I also discovered that there was a tremendous decline within the inner cities of Great Britain. There was desolation. As we saw earlier, the more well-to-do had moved out, leaving the poorer, aged and disadvantaged groups to fend for themselves. Some churches had closed down and others were only sustained by people who travelled in on Sundays and then retreated again to their nicer, middle-class suburbia. Thus the churches were becoming insulated from the real world – irrelevant to society especially in the context of the inner city; often inward-looking, self indulgent communities, lacking vision and passion for others. With little or no sense of mission, the Church has drifted into a maintenance mentality, while outside, the atmosphere of poverty and hopelessness spreads everywhere; the perfect soil for the seeds of wrong influences to be sown. So while the saints played church, enemy agents had a field day. Humanism, the occult, liberalism, existentialism, communism, per-missiveness, pluralism, just to name a few. Wicked men sowed evil while the saints slept. All this alarmed and distressed me, and I felt it was time that something positive was done.

CHAPTER TWENTY-ONE

And now . . .

In 1983, I attended a large Christian gathering in
Amsterdam, sponsored by the Billy Graham Evangel-
istic Association, much burdened by what I had
observed in England. I was concerned not only at the
many hurts and wrongs in society, and the alienation
between black and white even within the churches, but
at the fact that even when the will for reconciliation was
there, it was difficult in practical terms to achieve.

Because of their reception in this country, and the
problems of inherent English prejudice, many West
Indians have a very low self-image, and this carries over
into the church. For a long time the black church has
not really felt that their white brothers see them as
having a role and a purposeful contribution. Their
suspicion often has foundation. The white church can
often appear to have a superior attitude, reaching down
to their poorer black brothers rather than treating them
as equals. Often, in the past, just through lack of
thought, white Christians hurt their more sensitive
black brothers – by arranging inner city events without
involving them, and appearing to snub black pastors by
not including them on planning committees from the
beginning.

Within the West Indian Church there is much
fragmentation. Unlike the white church which until the
advent of the house-church movement was organised
along a set number of denominational lines, black

churches have developed independently of each other. There are some larger church networks such as the New Testament Assembly and the New Testament Church of God, but many more black churches are independent groupings of three or four congregations. This means there are no obvious and easy lines for communicating information to all black churches. To do so involves contacting many individual churches and groupings rather than ten or so large denominations as in the white church. This has even caused problems for black churches when they have wanted to work more closely with other black churches. In recent years white churches which have desired to reach out towards their black brothers in love and repentance have not found it easy. The black church system, by its very diversity seems an anomaly to the outsider. The black network is expansive. It is important to know the key individuals who can give an opening into a particular church or network of churches. Because there are so many networks it is very easy to ignore and overlook some simply out of ignorance rather than a deliberate act of discrimination.

On the one hand, the transformation of the white English churches due to the influence of the charismatic renewal has awakened concern both for those in the inner cities who are unemployed and deprived and also for a real expression of unity among the members of Christ's body. There is a growing awareness among some white church leaders of the need to repent of the former attitude of the Church towards West Indian Christians and to work in closer harmony with their black brethren.

Attitudes inherited from colonisation run deeper than many would imagine, requiring more than a repentance of prejudice towards those of other cultures. The English belief that they are superior is very deep rooted, an unconscious pride perhaps! On the other hand many black pastors are suspicious of the white hand of fellowship because behind it they still sense the English feeling of superiority. Some black pastors have not been to Bible college or received formal theological training, therefore it is easy for whites unwittingly to look down on them, or even, in some cases, to treat them patronisingly. The final insult is when they are accepted as mere tokens and not respected in their own right.

At the conference, I explained my concern for reconciliation to the leading evangelist Eric Delve, and I then met Clive Calver, the General Secretary of the British Evangelical Alliance. Once again, God was going before his servants, and Clive had been wondering for some time how the Evangelical Alliance could contact black Christians in Britain, but because of the difficulties outlined above, had not known how to set about it.

When I returned from Amsterdam, I gathered thirty or more Afro-Caribbean church leaders and discussed the problem of fragmentation among black-led churches and the polarisation between black and white Christian communities. Very frank and open discussions ensued. It was evident that my brothers were still hurting from events of the past and had grown very suspicious and fearful. This caused them to retreat into themselves and to pursue building their own churches and evangelising their own people. As we talked and prayed, tears flowed freely, and afterwards we decided to form the West Indian Evangelical Alliance to bring healing to our own fragmented community and to build bridges with white Christians. On 7th April 1984, the WIEA was born.

Back in London, I met again with Clive and with Brian Mills, the Prayer and Revival Secretary of the Evangelical Alliance, and we discussed the situation further. We were aware that the West Indian community was very fragmented, and, lacking a corporate identity, could not act with any kind of unity and so was powerless. Also, although Asian Christians and the Chinese and African churches had their own evangelical fellowships, the West Indians did not. And, as we have seen, even when white churches wished to work together with them and to propose a meeting or a joint project, there were practical difficulties of communication.

The West Indian Evangelical Alliance was given a further, formal launch in March 1985 in the presence of a large mixed congregation at Rye Lane chapel in Peckham, although it had already been functioning for almost a year. On this historic occasion, Brian Mills publicly apologised on behalf of the white evangelical community for "not treating our West Indian brethren as we should have done". He went on, "We need to repent of deep-seated prejudices and coldness of heart which have created distance between us, and to work out how our unity in Christ can find practical expression in the days ahead."

Selwyn Arnold, the overseer and bishop of the New Testament Church of God, was the main speaker who brought a very inspired message exhorting us to love and unity based on Christ's sacrifice, without compromising any of the essential truths of the gospel.

As the elected chairman of the WIEA, I spoke too, emphasising the need for black and white Christians to unite in order to become an authentic Christian witness in our torn and divided society. The specific aims of the WIEA were set out as follows:

* To strengthen relationships within the West Indian community thereby giving it a corporate identity.
* To build bridges between the West Indian and English communities.
* To become a voice for the nation representing the West Indian churches on social and spiritual matters.
* To encourage and equip leadership in the local

church by conducting consultations and seminars.
* To stimulate prayer and faith for renewal, restoration and revival.
* To mobilise the Church for evangelism.

Thus, in an evening of West Indian celebration with music from the New Testament Church Choir and the Mohabir Sisters (my daughters!), the West Indian Evangelical Alliance was launched. Already since its inception, communications are improving. WIEA is represented on the Council of Scripture Union, for example, and in general, major organisations are becoming aware of the need to include the black community and to weave them into the wider Christian scene, to the benefit of all. Although membership of a body like the WIEA does not come naturally to the West Indian mind, we are working to build up the concept of membership and of its importance in the long run.

The WIEA and the Evangelical Alliance together have also ventured into other fields, as in April 1987 when, together with the Department of Employment, they launched a joint programme aimed at generating employment and assisting those in areas of gross deprivation – a unique venture.

Dave Tomlinson, having provided accommodation for our family for eighteen months in Middlesbrough, felt God's leading to move his base to London. We too felt the need to be in London, and so at about the time of the launching of the WIEA we moved back to Brixton. Dave Tomlinson and his "Teamwork" co-workers continued to sponsor and support WIEA, for which it has also provided a base.

CHAPTER TWENTY-TWO

Closing the gap

There is a real need for partnership between black and white Christians. At a time when the nation is suffering so many divisions – between races, between north and south, male and female, rich and poor, employed and unemployed – the church needs to lead the way and set a precedent. Jesus can and does make a difference. Any true partnership must be based on a true knowledge of, and a genuine acceptance of one another.

The British Isles are now a multi-social, multi-cultural, multi-religious society. Peoples of all parts of the world find their roots in the streets of our major cities. The Empire which was flung to the far corners of the earth is now in reverse. The sons and daughters of colonialism whose grandparents were uprooted and transported as slaves and labourers across the seas are now returning to England as their home country, their motherland. These proud subjects of a crumbling Empire arise out of this rubble to claim a home and a future here in London which was once and still is their capital, their seat of Parliament, the home of their monarch.

1.5 million people from the Caribbean, 1.5 million from Africa, 3.5 million from Asia and South East Asia have already returned 'home'. Ten per cent of Britain's population is composed of these diverse ethnic groupings. They bring with them their religions, cultures, art-forms and life-styles. They build their temples and mosques as centres of their religious and social activities. There are now 1,200 mosques in England, 350 of which are in London, and there are plans to build a temple whose dome will be higher than that of St. Paul's Cathedral. To these shores have come the many different people who formed the British Empire. Many thousands came, during the war, and in the fifties and sixties. Twenty-five to thirty years after, we now have a second generation born here, having lived all their lives and never having seen the West Indies or Africa. They are actually British.

In the mid-fifties we came in the greatest numbers. Because of the work of the missionaries, many came as Christians of one or other denomination. This is especially true of the West Indians. Naturally, after the initial weather and culture shocks, they sought out their particular denomination for worship. Unfortunately, for some reason or other they were not made very welcome. Some found empty churches and a very cold conservative worship style while others were even asked not to return because the members were upset. The request was polite but definite. Discouraged and rejected, many were confused. Is this our Christian England which brought us the Gospel and the Church? Questions – too many questions. The result is that many rejected Christ and the Church and became agnostics or atheists, they were overthrown and their faith undermined.

However, others were determined that they would not allow anyone or any circumstance to rob them of their relationships with Jesus. They started to meet in homes to pray and encourage each other. They would pray, sing, preach and break bread. After a while these groups grew and soon they moved out of their front rooms into hired halls. It was not long after that they began to buy houses and redundant churches and to convert them into simple places of worship. These congregations formed a stable point for the growing West Indian community and provided many services to the aged, the young, the drop-outs of school and society, the single parents and also the voiceless minorities whose struggles are too numerous to take up here.

Out of their midst arose pastors and leaders who led their people with much courage, sacrifice and struggle. Now they are growing in number and have become a very significant force in the Christian scene. There are at least 150 groupings of churches with a constituency of 100 000 Christians. Three significant features of these churches are lively singing and worship, and straightforward and simple Bible preaching on the fundamentals. Their government and structures vary, but essentially revolve around a strong father-figure pastor and an elected board of deacons.

West Indians dress up to attend meetings and their women folk though well dressed do not use jewellery or heavy cosmetic colouring. Most of them wear a hat or scarf to meetings. As part of their devotion and separation to God they will abstain from sex outside of marriage and from attending shows in cinemas or theatres (although they do have televisions) and they avoid the use of alcohol and tobacco. Most of these churches will expect their members to be baptised in water and to speak in tongues. They will openly practise praying for the sick and casting out demons. Although at times they seem to be austere and authoritarian, those who spend time with them discover that there are some real trophies of grace, marvellous and miraculous conversions, astounding miracles and deliverances. Here are people who love God and Jesus seriously and yet radiate a joy and happiness that is contagious.

The tragedy is that all this development among black Christians remains unnoticed by the white Christian community and all that is happening among them. They exist in total isolation – neither wants to know. It seems as though the Church of God is practising its own peculiar brand of apartheid. Polarisation is encouraged, the gap and divide widens, barriers remain un-challenged – racial, cultural, and doctrinal barriers stand as dividing walls. The body of Christ is rent, torn and bleeding.

Most of the Afro-Caribbean immigrants settled in the inner cities, which in themselves constitute a problem of major proportions and present us with a very needy mission field. The inner city needs some further historical perspective. Permit me to use Brixton as an example, although I am sure that the parallels can be drawn in other areas.

Thirty years ago Brixton was a thriving centre of business and industry with a high rate of employment. It was a well-to-do middle-class area. The population had a sociological mix. There were intellectual student types, and professional workers of diverse skills involved in the building trade, factories and social services. Then the more well-to-do elements moved out and left the community without a heart. This situation worsened as new people moved into the area seeking accommo-dation and jobs. They were poor financially and had no natural links with their neighbours. They were strangers. The result – a community disconnected. Many, perhaps most, were from the Caribbean and were at one time being recruited from the various colonies to fill vacancies in the transport services and so on.

Two important factors which further contributed to the rupture of the community's life were, on the one hand, that the remaining indigenous white community felt threatened by this influx. They were totally unprepared to receive and accommodate people from a different culture. The problem was further emphasised because they were black. The warm welcome was missing. On the other hand the new immigrant population was equally unprepared, and so the adjustments that would lend themselves towards easy integration were absent. Tensions were generated as the effects of this spilled over in the shops, market places and schools. People's prejudices came into the open – the lack of cultural sensitivity on both sides contributed to the general feeling of intrusion on the one hand, and being unwanted on the other.

As far as I know, little was done at that time to take hold of this diversity and mould it into a cohesive community. The various strands were never woven into a fabric. The result is an impoverished society. It must be noted with great sadness that even the churches were unprepared and many of their members moved out leaving buildings empty and at the best of times functioning for a period as a migrant church – people travelling in for meetings and then leaving the area again. This meant that they could not sustain activities that might have contributed to the cohesion of the community or influenced it for God.

Over this period, the ethnic minorities were subjected to some very humiliating experiences. They became victims of discrimination which manifested itself in the pubs, at work, in schools, in places of entertainment, and also in the civil and social services. They were often harassed, abuse was hurled at them, they were even physically attacked. They were easy prey for un-scrupulous landlords, employers, and drug pushers. To deny that these things ever happened or to suggest that they were isolated incidents is naive to say the least, a failure to face reality and an unwillingness to address the real living fears and suspicions which followed as natural consequences.

Unfortunately, the vacuum that existed was filled by the wrong influences and elements in the society and this left the field free, preparing the soil for the wrong seeds to be sown. The elder generation blacks are still disillusioned, hurt and bleeding, while the younger generation blacks, especially those born here are saying that enough is enough. There is a sense of despair and depression and a feeling that there is very little hope for the future. What is more, they do not believe that anyone really cares.

No-one really listens to them. These and other factors compress and compel them into a ghetto situation which they do not want and which they fear but to which they are being driven because they feel insecure and unprotected. Not only are prejudices hardened, but despair is turned to anger and hostility. Over the same period and dating even further back a very important and wrong image of the blacks has been projected and perpetuated, that blacks cannot achieve great excellence and cannot be effective in management, education, politics, science, civil services and social services. It would appear as though they are forever destined to achieve so much but not more. The boundaries are already set. That they are good in sport and music but are underachievers in other fields is a myth promoted and perpetuated by literature, radio and TV shows. And the idea that they are unreasonable, given to violence and perpetrators of crime, is definitely not doing justice to them as a people. That there are criminal elements, radicals and activists among the blacks is as true as any other group within society but this negative image places an unbearable pressure on them. They resent it bitterly and it provokes very negative reactions. Something radical needs to be done urgently to correct this myth and this stereotyping.

Many blacks are made to feel like aliens and suffer a deep insecurity. They lack a real sense of belonging. Most of them have never seen a banana plant or coconut palm yet they are told to "Go home, you are not British." They cannot help wondering, "Who am I?" and feel themselves to be without roots, without homeland, not wanted. This is particularly tragic when one considers that these people were cruelly uprooted a few hundred years ago against their will and have never found a home since. An identity crisis! Maybe it was never anticipated but it happened nonetheless. They are portrayed as under-achievers. Their attainable goals are predetermined. They are expected to be satisfied with the goals prescribed and they are considered presumptuous if they aspire beyond those limits. The system, institutions, media and vested interests seem to be stacked against them and are designed to enforce and perpetuate that myth.

Blacks are readily and automatically blamed for civil disorders, social and moral decline in their communities, drug scenes, and the rising crime rate. All blacks are not innocent, but undue publicity is given to the unhealthy elements of this community, while insufficient positive presentation is given this people. The result is that they are held to ransom as a group for all that is wrong and cannot expect any justice. They are all tried and sentenced before the crime is committed. The lack of sufficient blacks in leadership positions in the police force, teaching professions and civil service leaves a great vacuum. They begin to accept that there is little or no value in trying. "We will never succeed." "It cannot be done," they think. There is a definite need to project and give more publicity and visibility to successful black people, such as businessmen, university professors and lecturers, lawyers, doctors, surgeons and so on. This will lift our sense of pride and morale, enhance our dignity and challenge our young people to aspire and aim for things other than sports, athletics and music. Unfortunately it must be said that some who have achieved high positions are often an embarrassment to their people, either because they have undergone a colour conversion, or because they represent minority interests only.

A lot of money is spent on the wrong things instead of on projects to further development and provide jobs.

Money is spent on research after research project, which gathers dust on shelves, and on umpteen clubs for fringe groups like homosexuals and lesbians. Most of these only aim at entertainment value and are merely cosmetic and irrelevant to the real needs of the average black person. They do not provide jobs and homes. Most of the black British are honest, hardworking, taxpaying, God-fearing, decent citizens who want to be left alone to make a success of their lives and a contribution to society. They refuse to get involved in schemes which they consider an insult to their intelligence, destructive to good morale and detrimental to their own values and quality of life. There is a whole army of black men and women who give invaluable and sacrificial voluntary labour to alleviate suffering, comfort, advise, encourage and correct. Many black pastors and youth workers who are in full-time secular employment have been carrying out full-time pastoral functions in their communities for the past twenty-five years. They receive no recognition and they are not even known, or often despised and maligned. Schemes and projects ought to exist that will release these people to exert their positive influence more fully.

So then, while there is calm, no effort should be spared to deal with the real causes of dissatisfaction. Radical steps should be taken to reduce the tension, to cool off the volcano now and not wait for it to erupt. Energies should be spent to change stereo-typed concepts and basic heart attitudes which will affect the economy and improve the quality of life for the majority. Too much is spent on too few and on the wrong things.

It is imperative that we explode the myths and correct the image of the black person in the nation. They should be seen as partners and not as parasites and problems. Educational programmes need to be launched to cater for those who for one reason or another dropped out of school early – education that is remedial but that also opens the doors to progressive development: the kind of programme that will qualify them for entering institutions of higher education. Schemes should be initiated that will identify, train and develop their skills in mechanics, carpentry, masonry, electronics and computers. There should be recruitment of blacks for the civil service, police force, teaching profession and other government institutions. It would be good to examine the reasons why this is not happening. Whatever happens blacks are not asking for a lowering of standards. It may be necessary to consider pre-training training.

There is a definite need to improve relationships between the police and the community. The task of the police is an unenviable one and unfortunately events of recent history are not all in their favour. However, there is still sufficient good will for a new initiative and sincere attempts need to be made to bridge this gap. People's confidence needs a boost. They do not ask that criminals escape justice, but that they do have much grounds for fear and suspicion.

In particular areas, there should be projects to encourage investment in the locality and to provide jobs, opportunities to work. Actually, this is one major factor from our perspective: jobs which in turn will provide the incentive to pursue other more long-term goals. There is also a need to provide funding that will release hardworking men and women to engage more fully in their particular endeavours to uplift the community. Men of integrity who will give positive input and be an influence for good.

Overall, there must be an atmosphere which suggests that somebody actually cares and is concerned about what happens to 'little me', to the unemployed, to single parents, to the aged. How this can be done I cannot fully see, but if a realistic approach can be found to implement a considerable programme it will do wonders to change the feeling in the air. Anything that

can be done to make the ethnic minorities feel that they
are British, and accepted; that they are needed and have
resources to contribute to the good of all. Academic
research papers or verbal reassurances will not suffice.
The approach has to be immensely pragmatic and
designed to reach people at grass roots.

On the positive side, there is much goodwill among
members of the black churches. Each community needs
a non-political group to function as a sounding board, as
agents for reconciliation and as initiators of projects in
their areas. We need independent agencies not formally
connected to the police, councils, or political parties, yet
in touch with real people and serving them, through
which black church members can influence the inner
city for good.

Constructive planning needs to go into creating
training schemes and development programmes which
are designed to attract the youth off the streets. These
should be locally based so that they can be seen and felt
and touched by residents. They will benefit the people
directly.

More black Christian leaders should be placed on our
school boards and other influential places in the
community.

Enlightened religious workers need to engage in more
deliberate actions to create a sense of community and
create a better understanding among the various
factions of divided society. There is much healing
needed in the community and the small number of
voluntary workers operating on shoe-string budgets
cannot turn this tide alone, it must be attempted on a
large scale.

Drug victims must be rehabilitated.

Existing organisations and related departments must
be renewed and revamped to provide a more friendly
and helpful, understanding and efficient service. I am
not an expert and am conscious that the professionals
may find much with which to disagree but may I be bold

enough to say that they have not got it all right either, although they have worked at it for many years and spent fortunes on various schemes. May I humbly suggest that it is possible for some simple common sense things to be done, to create a social revolution which will restore sound morals to our society, give hope to our people, and lay the foundations for the generation of tomorrow even if it means that we must reset our agendas.

For the leaders of the churches on both sides two important questions must be asked:

1 What validity has the message of the gospel in a world that is torn and divided? Are we any different? Have we got the Good News?

2 Can we remain silent and indifferent? Should we not reach out to bridge the gap, to effect reconciliation?

I appeal to all Christians, leaders and laymen alike of whatever ilk, denomination or race – let us make strenuous efforts for reconciliation. Surely Christ in us transcends the barriers which stand between us. However, reconciliation cannot be a cosmetic exercise and cannot be bought on the lowest common denominator. It must be based on reality. We cannot pretend love while prejudices dwell undealt with in our hearts. We cannot and should not feign oneness when we actually keep our distance and do not really want to know each other. We need to face up to real issues, first within ourselves and then with each other. Prejudice is not the monopoly of either white or black, we must look into ourselves and repent of this ugliness wherever it is found.

If reconciliation is to be effective, the following steps are necessary:

We need to forgive the hurts, ill-treatment and prejudices which lie buried in our history and in the present – to offer forgiveness and healing to one another.

We need to repent of the things which have caused so much hurt and pain, so that we ourselves may be released and in so doing, release others.

We must respect and accept one another as equals, meet and visit each other on equal terms on home territory without requiring that the one become the other in order to be accepted.

Go to the others. Reach out. Reconciliation means dying, embracing the cross, especially in the case of black Christians, who will hardly now want to come to their white brothers if for no reason other than the fear of rejection the second time round.

On a one to one basis, go out and with much prayer and perseverance make friends with your neighbours in the name of Jesus's love, which is in you. And how about rural and suburban churches linking up with their poorer brethren in the inner cities?

For too long we have abandoned our responsibility to society and retreated into a spiritual cocoon, into the safety and security of a so-called spiritual world, and left the secular field open for demons to work through evil and wicked men to dictate the pace, formulate and initiate diabolical philosophies, and institute systems which motivate and mould the actions and thinking of our generation in the field of religion, government, education, art, culture, politics, social welfare, commerce and industry. Isn't it time that we Christians, black and white, arise to reclaim the territories we surrendered to the enemy?

Europe and Britain can no longer be conceived as white only. Britain now has citizens and subjects who have no other home but here. This nation, our generation, will never forgive us if we fail them by ignoring this need, the challenge to build bridges and effect reconciliation. We ignore it to our peril and shame. Let us be brothers – RECONCILED.